A Culinary History of

MISSOURI

A Culinary History of
MISSOURI

FOODWAYS & ICONIC DISHES OF THE SHOW-ME STATE

SUZANNE CORBETT
& DEBORAH REINHARDT

AMERICAN PALATE

Published by American Palate
A Division of The History Press
Charleston, SC
www.historypress.com

First published 2021

Manufactured in the United States

ISBN 9781467150361

Library of Congress Control Number: 2021941053

CONTENTS

ACKNOWLEDGEMENTS

I t is with gratitude that we offer this hearty huzzah for all of those who helped bring a taste of Missouri's food history, along with its related recipes, to this project. We raise a glass to toast these individuals, while asking forgiveness for any oversights: Andy Hahn, executive director, Campbell House Museum; John Hoover, executive director, St. Louis Mercantile Library; Toby Carrig and Mary Elise Okenfuss, Ste. Geneviève Tourism; Sara Hodge, curator, Herman T. Pott National Inland Waterways Library; Nicholas Fry, curator, John W. Barriger III National Railroad Library; Derek Klaus, director of communications, Visit KC; Carolyn Wells, Kansas City Barbeque Society; Susan Wade, public relations manager, Springfield Convention and Visitors Bureau; Daniel Johnson, executive director, Robidoux Row Museum; Marci Bennett, executive director, St. Joseph Convention & Visitors Bureau; Liz Coleman, communications manager, Missouri Division of Tourism; Isobel McGowan, Shakespeare Chateau; Jim Pallone and Jeff Keyasko, J C Wyatt House; Cierra Monsees, Missouri State Fair; Brian Lookout, Osage Nation/Ah Tha Tse Catering; Rich LoRusso, LoRusso's Cucina; Monsignor Salvadore Polizzi, Hill Historian; Patty Held, Patty Held Wine Consulting; Nick Sacco, park ranger, and Julie Northrip, interpretation, education and volunteer program manager, Ulysses S. Grant National Historic Site; David Newmann, interpretation program manager, Ste. Geneviève National Historic Park; Doug Harding, park ranger, Gateway Arch National Park; Adam Criblez, associate professor, Southeast Missouri State University; Linda Williams, Windrush Farm Arts & Plants; Chef Rob

Connoley, Bulrush Restaurant; Corrina Smith, executive director, Columbia Farmers' Market; TaylorAnn Washburn, marketing specialist, Missouri Wine and Grape Board; Laura Burns and Frank Romano, the Parkmoor Drive-In; and photographer Jim Corbett III.

Many thanks to our acquisitions editor, Chad Rhoad, and the team at The History Press for their expertise and support. Finally, to our families, thank you for allowing us to be storytellers and supporting us over the years with your love and patience.

INTRODUCTION

Anyone who came to Missouri could never claim that they left hungry. Since the state's earliest beginnings, Missouri's tables have been filled with a bountiful collection of food and drink. This book explores many of those foods, while offering a taste of Missouri via its foodways and recipe collection. This savory history celebrates cooks and chefs, brewers and winemakers, those who bottle soda and those who pour spirits. From the earliest colonial tables in Ste. Geneviève to family farms and feasting on signature foods like Kansas City barbecue and St. Louis Gooey Butter Cake, we hope this book encourages you to discover a cuisine that Missourians have been eating up for more than two hundred years. Allow us to show you to your table.

Chapter 1

NATIVE BOUNTY AND THE COLONIAL TABLE

When baking bread, it helps to have good mud. Good mud mixed with the right amount of straw to build a mud oven. This was a common oven found throughout Missouri during the early colonial period, and it yielded the diet mainstay for the colonial French, Missouri's first European settlers.

Bread was baked from flour milled from the wheat the colonists grew—a product that complemented the natural abundance of foods that attracted not only the Europeans but also native inhabitants to migrate to what would become the state of Missouri.

Missouri's abundant resources revolved around its ability to provide reliable food sources, which afforded food security for its settlements. These settlements included Missouri's earliest residents, the moundbuilding Mississippians and Native American tribes—people who enjoyed a cornucopia of easily foraged, gathered and cultivated indigenous foods, supplemented by hunters who harvested a seemingly unlimited supply of game, birds and fish. These were proteins native cooks could roast, stew or dry for future use. These foods could be traded to neighboring tribes as well as French explorers/traders and colonialists who permanently settled along the Mississippi's western shore and its connecting tributaries.

Native Foods to Colonial Foodways

Missouri's woodlands were a hunter-gatherer paradise. Game, fish and forest delicacies such as black walnuts, persimmons, pawpaws and pecans were eaten. To enhance the food supply, beans, squash and corn were cultivated by the semi-nomadic Illini, Quapaw, Chickasaw and Oto tribes, as well as Missouri's predominant tribes, the Missouria and Osage. These indigenous foods are best described as a frontier smorgasbord for the French colonists, who, by luck, stumbled on economic and culinary good fortune when they settled in one of the most fertile regions in the country.

This region is known as Upper Louisiana and the Illinois Country— an area whose rich soil and terroir produced the finest wheat, yielding bumper crops that, in turn, drove the establishment of lucrative milling operations that exported 300,000 pounds of flour to New Orleans in 1738 and 1739. This stone-ground whole wheat flour produced a dense bread that villagers reportedly ate nearly three pounds of per day; they were also used as edible trenchers.

Wheat, milled into flour, provided a valuable commodity that colonists traded for imported food staples and luxury items such as sugar, coffee and French wines—a favorite for those weary of local wines made from native grapes and a welcomed addition to the table.

Another valuable export was bear meat and bear grease, the latter an essential for cooking and preservation. Gourmands of the day favored bear hams, extolling their superior taste over hams produced from locally raised hogs. This hot commodity unfortunately depleted Missouri's black bear population. It would take more than two hundred years for the black bear to return to Missouri and regain numbers to a level where the Missouri Department of Conservation would approve limited bear hunting.

Missouri buffalo and elk suffered fates similar to the black bear. Their numbers also dwindled; the buffalo were pushed beyond their Missouri range, and elk were completely wiped out. Another delicacy that suffered from overharvesting was the pelican, once abundantly found along the river. This tasty bird, like the black bear, has also reestablished itself along the upper Mississippi River. Luckily, quail, prairie hen, partridge, crane, duck, geese, wild pigeon, grouse and doves remained in fairly good supply. However, when needed, to supplement the food supply Shawnee hunters provided deer and turkey to the settlements.

While game and local livestock contributed greatly to the daily diet, cooks added variety to the menu with fresh fish, river mussels and

Pawpaws' soft custard pulp and tropical flavor, best described as banana, explains its nickname, the "Missouri banana." *Missouri Department of Conservation.*

After overharvesting by colonists, the black bear, which disappeared for more than 150 years, has returned to Missouri. *Missouri Department of Conservation.*

freshwater shellfish. A favorite catch was catfish—in French *barbue*, which means bearded. Descriptions of dishes featuring this bearded fish occasionally appear in diaries and letters of the period. One such account described a popular Friday night specialty: catfish smothered in sour sorrel seasoned with pepper and sufficient salt. An elegant dish for its time, it illustrates Missouri's French Creole culinary prowess, confirming their culinary expertise, about which Henry Brackenridge wrote in his 1834 account *Reflections of the West*: "[T]he humblest of French cooks possessed an appreciation of the culinary arts and a mastery of cookery."

This appreciation elevated colonial cooks above others, which also included the enslaved Africans who arrived with the French. They expanded the area's culinary diversity and reputation and are credited with introducing new foods such as okra and gumbos.

Unlike other American colonial groups, Missouri's French defined themselves through their foodways. Illustrated by more than cooking and baking skills, households made a sizable investment in cookware and tableware. Inventories and shipping manifests document the importance and interest in setting a table. Among the listed items were faience (ceramic dinnerware), etched glassware and fine silver service pieces. These items were considered necessary to ensuring the continuance of French culinary

Pewter, tablecloths and ceramic dinnerware, including French faience, illustrate the 1790s dining table of the successful Ste. Geneviève merchant Louis Bolduc. *Ste. Geneviève Tourism.*

traditions and the fostering of a civilized table. While the social elite possessed more table finery, poor households compensated by elevating their tables by utilizing the finest-quality foods and luxury ingredients they could afford.

No matter the dishes used to set the table, whether the household was poor or rich, equal importance was placed on a cook's tools. Kitchens were stocked with an array of cooking implements—kettles and pots made from iron, tin, copper and wood. Specialty baking pans, pudding molds, braziers, wooden bread troughs and pepper mills were all common implements used.

Forks were usually made of steel instead of pewter, which was too soft. Early inventories revealed few table knives, if any, suggesting that personal hunting knives were used or that food was served precut or pulled apart at the table. Individual place settings slowly became an affordable norm, replacing the communal pot or trencher placed in the center of the table.

Common Foods, Common Fields

Common fields provided open prairies to grow crops, harvest firewood and graze livestock. Ste. Geneviève's Le Grand Champ, the "Big Field," is still visible on the edge of the city. One of St. Louis's common fields reached south to the border of another French village, Carondelet. These common fields cultivated a variety of row crops. Cabbage, carrots, eggplant, okra, sweet peas, herbs, greens, beans, tomatoes, squash, beans and corn were grown. However, corn was primarily used as stock feed and was eaten by the enslaved and the landless as well as when wheat was scarce—during one such shortage, the French lamented being reduced to eating cornbread.

As more groups migrated into Missouri, each brought new crops, expanding the menu. Seed potatoes arrived from Pennsylvania around 1770. Apple orchards were among the first crops established by the French Canadians to provide the main ingredient for sweet and hard ciders and tarts.

Hogs, cattle and poultry grazed in the common fields, freely foraging, as well as roamed through the streets, forcing residents to build stockades to protect home gardens and property. Of the domestic livestock, pork was a preferred meat. Milk cattle were prized for cream and butter, essential ingredients for the apple tarts and pastries the French loved.

While the apple orchards flourished, wild strawberries, mulberries, persimmons, red and yellow prairie plums, pawpaws and wild grapes continued to be gathered. Wild pecans, which grew in thick groves found

Above: The 1808 Bequette Ribault House still overlooks Ste. Geneviève's Le Grand Champ (the Big Field), where crops were cultivated. *Jim Corbett III.*

Left: Wild pecans, a delicacy favored by Missouri's colonists, are still available in southeast Missouri, packaged as the Creole treat maple sugared pecans. *Jim Corbett III.*

along the Mississippi, were particularly prized. Unfortunately, by 1811, overharvesting had destroyed the pecan groves along the St. Louis riverfront. Wild pecans have survived in Ste. Geneviève, with some trees dating to the colonial period. Wild pecans have black stripes and are less than half the size of commercially grown pecans. Wild pecans are still harvested and sold in Ste. Geneviève to locals and the tourist trade.

On the Menu

Missouri's French Creole cooks understood that cooking was an art. They were seldom afraid to explore new foods and delighted in the cooking of vegetables, soups, stews, fricassees and gumbos. Of course, the wealthier the family, the bigger the menu. A Sunday dinner for the well-to-do Lewis Bolduc family, whose "poteaux sur sole" (post on sill) vertical log home is preserved as a museum today, could have easily included a vegetable soup whose main ingredient depended on what was in season or stored in the cellar; catfish, pan-fried in refined bear oil; homemade boudin sausages; roast pig; and desserts ranging from fresh fruit tarts and candies to maple-sugared pecans.

Sugared pecans and pralines were among those local confections that used the native pecans. Croquignoles—a buttery fried pastry drizzled with honey, syrup or sprinkled with maple sugar—were a must-have on celebration menus.

Meals were often washed down with Spanish or French wines, local beer, ciders and brandies, after which coffee was served, if available. As for hard liquor, rum was the easiest hard spirit to obtain, as it was sourced in the Caribbean and shipped from New Orleans, Louisiana.

Food and Celebrations

Observing how the colonial French celebrated holidays, Thomas Sharf wrote, "The French were so devout they celebrated every feast and so fun loving they wished there were twice as many to celebrate."

Celebrations were food-focused, especially during Christmas with le Réveillon, a sumptuous feast held after Christmas Eve Mass. Households would plan their le Réveillon feast by setting the table with the best foods possible. Menus often featured whole roasted pig, game birds and tourtieres

Le Réveillon, the traditional sumptuous feast held after Christmas Eve Mass, is re-created annually at the Felix Vallé House, a Missouri State Historic Site. *Ste. Geneviève Tourism.*

(meat pies), in addition to Le Réveillon's "thirteen sweets," which represented the twelve disciples and the Christ child. Among the sweet thirteen that could have been included were croquignoles, pralines, apple pastries, fondant candies and preserved fruit.

Holiday parties culminated with Epiphany, the old Twelfth Night, which closes the Christmas season and kicks off the pre-Lenten season of Carnival. Twelfth Night revolved around the serving of the King's Cake, a fanciful cake enriched with butter, incorporating aromatic spices, ground nuts and fruit glaze. The recipe has drastically changed over the years to its present New Orleans incarnation, a yeasted and raised sweet bread covered in colored sugars with a small plastic baby representing the baby Jesus baked inside.

A toy baby was never baked into a French colonial King's Cake. Instead, its hidden treasure was a bean that was placed in the batter before being baked. During the Twelfth Night Ball, the King's Cake was served first to all the gentlemen. The gentleman who finds the bean is proclaimed king, and the new king chooses a queen. The royal couple is expected to appear at social and community functions throughout the year. The king's final obligation is to host the next year's ball.

Other recipes prepared during festivals, especially during winter, included pancakes made on Shrove Tuesday (Fat Tuesday). Made with a batter enriched with eggs, milk and flour, the recipe was designed to use up the surplus of household eggs and milk, ingredients restricted during the Lenten fast. Theses pancakes are thin, resembling crepes, and were fried in a long-handled pan in the hearth or atop a platform stove. Fat Tuesday pancakes promised good luck to the maker who could successfully flip their pancake over while still in the pan without having it drop into the fire.

COLONIAL SITES TO EXPLORE AND SAVOR

Ste. Geneviève's colonial culture and cuisine are celebrated at a number of historic sites and properties, many of which now compose the Ste. Geneviève National Historical Park, operated by the National Park Service.

Among those culinary outposts to explore is the 1790 Green Tree Tavern. Operated as a tavern, inn and gathering place, Green Tree Tavern is the oldest vertical log building in the area. Another building that is a few years younger than Green Tree is the Bolduc House, a National Historic Landmark. Considered the crown jewel of the four properties operated and maintained by the Centre for French Colonial Life, Bolduc House is renowned for its gallery, summer kitchen, gardens and interpretive programing.

Le Grand Champ, the Big Field, is located south of the historic district, bordering St. Mary's Road. The common fields are still visible and cultivated. Each October, the old common field becomes the site for Ste. Geneviève's annual Rural Heritage Day. This event presents early nineteenth-century farming, harvesting and cooking demonstrations along with folkways artisans.

Across from the Big Field are three surviving vertical log structures, including the Bequette-Ribault House, built in 1808. A restoration masterpiece overseen by Chaumette Vineyard & Winery owner Hank Johnson, it accurately reflects the period and features original architectural elements, such as its impressive stone hearth. Another restored outbuilding serves as a hospitality center for Bequette Ribault House and tasting bar for Chaumette Vineyards.

The Felix Vallé House, designed as a combination mercantile store and residence, is a Federal-style limestone structure reflecting American architectural influences that came to Missouri after the Louisiana Purchase. Vallé bought the property in 1824 and used it as a home and mercantile storefront for his trading company, Menard & Vallé, selling housewares and

After nearly three hundred years, La Guignolée, the colonial French New Year's Eve party, is still celebrated in eighteenth-century style in Ste. Geneviève, Missouri. *Ste. Geneviève Tourism.*

other goods supplied by the steamboat trade. Le Réveillon and an 1820s picnic are among the Vallé site's special events where food is the centerpiece of the interpretive program.

La Guignolée, Missouri's original New Year Eve party, is an event that encourages one to party like it's 1769. The event is practiced much as it was three hundred years ago in Ste. Geneviève and other surviving villages such as Old Mines. The night features the La Guignolée singers, costumed revelers who go door to door singing and dancing, seeking handouts of food and drink. Today, La Guignolée takes place in the streets, cafés and taverns of Ste. Geneviève's Historic District and is open to the public. Everyone is welcome to ring in the New Year and follow the La Guignolée singers or wait for their arrival at the watch party, held at the French Colonial America's Centre for French Colonial Life and the Bolduc House.

Plan to return for Twelfth Night Ball or King's Ball, held on the first Saturday closest to January 6. These balls are staged on both sides of the Mississippi along the French corridor of Illinois and Missouri. Because of the competition, Ste. Geneviève holds a King's Ball on the first Saturday of February. It is a ticketed event open to the public, who are encouraged to arrive in colonial dress (although this not required).

Old Mines, a colonial destination predating Ste. Geneviève and established as a French mining settlement, is located under an hour northwest of Ste. Geneviève. Old Mines, together with its historic society, actively preserves its foodways, music and the eighteenth-century French dialect, called "pawpaw French"—a cultural trio visitors can enjoy the first weekend in October during the Fete d'Automné.

The Museum at the Gateway Arch, located beneath the Gateway Arch, provides a look at colonial St. Louis. The museum's colonial gallery presents the foodways of Missouri's native people and its French settlers via interactive exhibits on French colonial cooking. The museum also hosts free special events throughout the year, including an Afternoon Twelfth Night Ball held on a Saturday afternoon. Visitors can learn colonial dances, enjoy eighteenth-century French music and sample period desserts, which include a slice of King's Cake.

St. Charles, Missouri, founded four years after St. Louis in 1769 as the Les Petites Cotes (the Little Hills), became San Carlos del Misuri (St. Charles of the Missouri) when the Spanish took procession. Lewis and Clark began their westward expedition from the St. Charles landing. Just eighteen years

The King's Cake is the centerpiece at the Gateway Arch Museum's Twelfth Night Ball, a free event that includes a slice of the cake. *Suzanne Corbett.*

later, St. Charles became Missouri's first state capital. The first capital buildings are now a Missouri State Historic Site. Consider taking a tour and strolling the brick-lined Main Street, where some of its shops and eateries are housed in buildings dating to the late 1700s and early 1800s. Lewis and Clark—as well as another famous migrant who would settle in Missouri, Daniel Boone—may well have visited these sites.

RECIPES

The following recipes, unless noted otherwise, are based on period recipes dating to the eighteenth and early nineteenth centuries. Each recipe has been updated for the twenty-first-century cook and can be successfully prepared using a modern stovetop or an open hearth.

French Colonial Cracked Wheat Bread

2 cups whole wheat flour
½ cup cracked wheat
2 packages dry yeast
2 cups warm water (120 degrees F)
1 tablespoon coarse salt
½ cup wildflower honey
½ cup melted butter
2 to 3 cups all-purpose flour

1. In a large mixing bowl combine whole wheat flour, cracked wheat and yeast.
2. Stir in water and salt, then add honey, butter and enough flour to make a stiff dough.
3. Turn out on a floured surfaced and knead until smooth. This takes about 5 to 8 minutes.
4. Place in a lightly buttered bowl, cover with a towel and allow to rise until doubled. Punch down dough, divide in half and shape into round loaves.
5. Place on a greased baking sheet and allow to rise until doubled again.
6. Heat oven to 375 degrees F. Bake for 35 minutes or until dough sounds hollow when tapped on bottom (190 to 200 degrees internal temperature). Makes 2 loaves.

No-Knead French Bread

4 cups unbleached bread flour
1 tablespoon coarse salt
1 cup warm water or ale
1 tablespoon dry yeast
2 tablespoons sugar
1 cup warm whole milk

1. Place bread flour and salt in a large mixing bowl.
2. Mix together the warm water, yeast and sugar in a separate bowl. Allow mixture to set until it begins to look foamy. This is also referred to as a sponge.
3. Combine milk with the yeast mixture and pour into the flour.
4. Lightly combine together using a spoon or your fingers. Mix just enough to make a dough (this dough will be sticky).
5. Cover and allow dough to raise until doubled.
6. Remove dough from bowl and place on a lightly floured surface. Gather dough into a ball and pat out into a circle. Fold each dough circle in half, then turn the dough and fold into thirds.
7. Heat oven to 400 degrees F. Place folded loaf on a baking sheet sprinkled with coarse cornmeal. Allow to rise until doubled.
8. Bake for 30 to 35 minutes, until nicely browned and the loaf sounds hollow when tapped on the bottom. Internal temperature should be between 190 and 200 degrees. Makes 1 large loaf.

Pain Perdu ("Lost Bread")

4 eggs
1 cup cream
2 tablespoons brandy
Nutmeg to taste
Butter
1 small loaf firm bread, sliced (about 10 to 12 slices)
Maple syrup

1. In a large bowl, whisk together eggs, cream, brandy and nutmeg. Set aside.
2. Place a heavy skillet over medium heat. Add enough butter to the skillet to generously cover the bottom.
3. Dip bread slices into egg mixture, a few at a time. Place in bottom of the skillet and brown on each side.
4. Remove and keep warm. Repeat with the remaining bread slices, adding more butter as needed to skillet to finish frying all the bread.
5. Serve lost bread with maple syrup and extra butter. Makes 4–6 servings.

Osage Fry Bread
Recipe courtesy Osage Nation.

4 cups all-purpose flour
1 teaspoon salt
2 tablespoons baking powder
2 cups milk or water, warmed
1 tablespoon melted shortening
Oil for frying

1. In a large bowl combine flour, salt and baking powder.
2. Combine the warmed milk (or water) with the melted shortening and stir into flour.
3. Gently knead dough on a lightly flour surface until it holds together to form a ball.
4. Pat or roll dough out to about 1-inch thickness. Cut into 2-inch squares.
5. Cut a slit in the center of each square. Set aside.
6. Pour an inch of oil into a heavy skillet and heat over medium heat (350 degrees F).
7. Fry dough squares a few at a time until golden on each side. This takes only a few minutes on each side.
8. Remove from oil using a slotted spoon and place on paper towels to drain. Makes about 2 dozen.

Osage Meat Pies
(Based on a recipe from the Osage Nation)

2 pounds coarse ground beef
1 cup finely diced suet or shortening
Black pepper and salt to taste
1 cup water
3 to 4 ramps (wild onions) or green onions, finely chopped
Fry bread dough
Foil

1. In a mixing bowl, combine beef, suet, salt, pepper, water and ramps.
2. Divide fry bread dough into 2-inch sized balls.
3. Roll each dough ball to a ¼-inch thickness and cut into 8-inch circles.
4. Spread ½ cup meat filling in the center of each dough circle.
5. Moisten edges of dough with a little water and then fold dough over meat. Seal by pinching the edges shut or pressing edges together using a fork.
6. Place pies seam side down on a lightly greased or parchment-lined baking sheet.
7. Heat oven to 425 degrees F and bake pies for 20 minutes, until crusts have browned and meat filling has cooked through, reached an internal temperature of 160 degrees.
8. Remove meat pies from oven and cool for 15 minutes. Loosely wrap pies in foil to keep warm. Makes about a dozen pies. Yield can vary depending on the size made.

Dried Red Corn Stew
Recipe courtesy Osage Nation.

2 cups dried red or white corn
6 cups water
1 pound short ribs or a meaty ham hock
1 large onion, chopped
Coarse salt and pepper to taste

1. Place corn in a large stockpot, cover with cold water and allow to soak overnight.
2. Drain corn and return to stockpot.
3. Add water, meat, onion, salt and pepper.
4. Bring back to a boil and then reduce heat and simmer until meat and corn are tender.
5. Remove the short ribs from stew.
6. Separate the meat from the bones. Discard bones and return meat to stew.
7. Season to taste with salt, pepper and dried chile, if desired. Makes 8 servings.

Jerky

1 pound lean, thinly sliced red meat (venison, buffalo or beef)*
Coarse salt
Cracked pepper
Liquid smoke

1. Place a layer of sliced meat in 9-inch square or round shallow dish.
2. Sprinkle lightly and evenly with salt, pepper and liquid smoke.
3. Repeat, adding another layer of meat and spices as in the first layer.
4. Cover with a piece of parchment paper or plastic wrap.
5. Weigh down wrapped meat using a plate or a few empty canning jars and refrigerate overnight.
6. Using a broiler pan or baking pan fitted with a rack, layer meat on top of rack. Do not overlap meat. If necessary, use two pans.
7. Place in a 250-degree oven for 3½ to 4 hours, or until meat is completely dry.
8. Remove jerky from oven and cool. Store in airtight containers in a refrigerator. Recipe yields about 1 pound of jerky.

*For a crisper jerky, cut meat across the grain. For a chewier jerky, cut meat with the grain.

Persimmon Bread

2 cups flour
1 teaspoon salt
1 teaspoon baking soda
½ teaspoon grated nutmeg
½ cup butter
1 cup sugar
2 eggs
1 ½ cups persimmon puree
1 cup chopped black walnuts, pecans or hickory nuts
¼ cup brandy

1. Heat oven to 350 degrees F.
2. Grease a 9x5-inch loaf pan.
3. In a mixing bowl, sift together flour, salt, baking soda and nutmeg.
4. In another large mixing bowl, combine butter and sugar and cream together until fluffy.
5. Add eggs to butter mixture, one at a time, followed by the persimmon puree.
6. Add flour mixture and blend until smooth, then fold in nuts and brandy. Spoon batter into prepared loaf pan.
7. Bake for 60 minutes or until a wooden pick inserted in the center comes out clean.
8. Remove from oven and allow to cool for 10 minutes before removing bread from pan. Allow to cool completely on wire rack. Makes 1 large loaf or 2 to 3 small loaves.

Black Walnut Biscuits
Recipe inspired by period recipes and Hammons Black Walnuts.

1 cup brown sugar
½ cup butter
1 large egg
1 tablespoon vanilla (optional)
1 ¾ cups flour
1 teaspoon salt

1 teaspoon baking soda
1½ cups black walnut pieces

1. Heat oven to 350 degrees F.
2. In a large bowl, cream together brown sugar and butter until fluffy.
3. Add egg and vanilla and mix until smooth.
4. Mix together flour, salt and baking soda. Add into butter/sugar mixture and fold in black walnuts.
5. Drop by rounded teaspoonfuls onto a greased or parchment-lined baking sheet.
6. Bake 8 to 10 minutes for a softer texture or 12 to 15 minutes for a crisper cookie. Makes about 2½ dozen.

Pawpaw Pudding

1 cup sugar
1 cup whole milk or half and half
2 eggs
2 tablespoons flour
¼ teaspoon salt
1 teaspoon ginger
1 teaspoon allspice
1½ cups pawpaw pulp

1. Heat oven to 350 degrees F.
2. Combine the sugar, milk, eggs, flour, salt, spices and pawpaw pulp together in a large bowl. Mix until smooth.
3. Pour into a lightly buttered 1½-quart baking dish. For individual servings, 6 small ramekins or custard cups can be used. (Pudding can also be poured into unbaked pie shell and baked.)
4. Place the filled baking dishes in the oven and bake for 30 to 35 minutes or until pudding is set. Note that the ramekins will bake faster than the larger pudding.
5. When puddings are set, remove from oven and cool. Refrigerate until ready to serve.
6. Serve with whipped cream or dusted with powdered sugar. Makes 6 servings.

Catfish Gumbo

½ cup flour
½ cup oil or butter
2 cups chopped onions
½ cup green peppers
½ cup chopped celery
3 cloves garlic
2 cups chopped tomatoes
4 cups chopped okra
1 pound of boneless catfish, cut into chunks
Salt and pepper to taste
Steamed rice
Chopped green onions

1. In a large stockpot, combine the flour and oil/butter. Heat over a low to medium heat.
2. Whisk the butter and flour, also called a roux, until golden dark brown. This will take about 15 to 20 minutes, depending on the kind of stockpot used and the intensity of the heat. For example, a cast-iron skillet, which holds heat well, will brown the roux a little quicker.
3. Sauté the onions, peppers, celery, garlic and tomatoes in the roux until onions are tender.
4. Place okra in a bowl and cover with water, then add with the catfish to the sautéed vegetables. Season with salt and pepper.
5. Simmer, uncovered, for 50 to 60 minutes, allowing the broth to reduce and the mixture to become thick.
6. Before serving, adjust seasonings one last time, adding salt and pepper. Dried hot red peppers can be added at this time if a spicier dish is preferred. Serve over steamed rice, garnished with chopped green onions. Makes 6 servings.

Maple Sugared Wild Pecans

*1 pound shelled, halved wild Missouri pecans**
½ cup real maple syrup
Coarse salt

1. Place a heavy cast-iron skillet over a medium heat.
2. Mix pecans and maple syrup together, then add to the skillet over a medium heat.
3. Stir to promote even glazing, which will also help prevent burning.
4. Stir until the maple syrup caramelizes and the pecans are lightly toasted.
5. Remove pecans from the skillet and spread them out on a piece of parchment paper to cool. Lightly salt to taste. Makes 6 to 8 servings

*Any other kind of pecan can be substituted.

Poulet Poche Au Vin Blanc

2 carrots, peeled and cut into 1½- or 2-inch pieces
2 leeks, washed, cut into 1-inch slices (use only the white and light green stalk of the leek)
⅓ cup chopped lovage or celery leaves
¼ cup butter
2½-pounds whole chicken, washed dried and cut into serving pieces
Coarse salt
10 to 12 peppercorns, crushed
1½ cups white wine
1½ cups chicken stock or water
4 sprigs each of parsley, thyme and tarragon, tied together to form an herb bouquet
2 tablespoons flour mixed with ¼ cup water or white wine

1. In a large cast-iron Dutch oven, sauté the carrots, leeks and lovage/celery in butter over medium-high heat for about 5 to 8 minutes, until carrots are barely tender.
2. Place chicken on top of the vegetables and season to taste with salt and pepper.
3. Brown chicken and then pour in wine, stock and herb bouquet.

4. Reduce heat to low. Cover and simmer until chicken is tender.
5. Remove chicken to a serving plate and keep warm.
6. Strain cooking liquid and return to the cookpot. Whisk in the flour/water and cook until juices have thickened. Season to taste with salt and pepper and additional fresh parsley, thyme or tarragon, if desired. Makes 4 servings.

Flat Apple Tart

Pastry:
½ cup butter
1 ½ cups flour
Dash of salt
1 egg
¼ cup cold water

Filling:
4 to 5 cooking apples, peeled and sliced
¼ cup honey
1 egg white, lightly beaten
Raw sugar

1. In a mixing bowl, cut the butter into the flour and salt.
2. In a separate bowl, whisk together the egg and cold water.
3. Add egg mixture into flour mixture and mix into a ball. Chill dough.
4. Roll out into a 12-by-14-inch rectangle about ¼-inch thick.
5. Place pastry on a lightly greased or parchment-lined baking sheet.
6. Arrange apples on half of the pastry and drizzle with honey.
7. Pull pastry over apples and pinch dough to seal. Cut a few steam vents into top of pastry.
8. Brush top with a beaten egg white and lightly sprinkle with raw sugar.
9. Bake at 375 degrees F for 30 minutes or until apples are tender and pastry has browned.
10. Remove from oven and cool. Makes 8 servings.

Pork and Apple Tourtiere

3 slices bacon, finely chopped
1 ½ cups finely chopped onion
1 pound ground fresh pork
2 cups peeled and chopped apples
1 teaspoon thyme leaves
Salt and black pepper to taste
1 teaspoon nutmeg
¼ cup flour
Pastry for a two-crust pie
1 egg, beaten

1. In a large skillet placed over a medium heat, cook bacon until it just begins to brown.
2. Add the onions and sauté until tender and golden, about 10 minutes.
3. Add the ground pork and cook until no traces of pink remain, about 5 minutes.
4. Drain off excess liquid from meat and then stir in the apples, thyme, salt, pepper and nutmeg.
5. Transfer the pork mixture to a shallow bowl. Cover and refrigerate until cooled. Filling is best chilled before adding it to the pastry case.
6. Heat oven to 400 degrees F. Roll out pastry and line the bottom of a 9-inch pie plate or cake pan with one of the pastry crusts.
7. Remove filling from refrigerator and mix in the ¼ cup flour. Add filling to the pastry-lined pan. Place the remaining crust on top. Seal and crimp pastry edges together.
8. Make several small decorative slits in the top crust for venting. Before baking, brush top with crust with beaten egg to promote a deeper brown crust.
9. Bake for 35 to 45 minutes until the crust is golden. Makes one pie, yielding 6 servings.

Cherry Bounce

2 quarts sour red cherries, stems removed
8 cups sugar
4 quart-size canning jars, clean
4 cinnamon sticks
1 teaspoon whole cloves
8 cups brandy, rum or whiskey

1. Divide the cherries and sugar equally among canning jars.
2. Place a cinnamon stick and a few whole cloves in each jar and cover the cherries with liquor.
3. Clean off jar rims and seal.
4. Place in a dark, cool place and allow to age for three months.
5. When ready to serve, strain bounce, reserving the cherries, which will be easy to pit, for use in desserts, cocktails or a topping for ice cream. Makes about 2 quarts of bounce.

Pecan Pralines

1 ½ cups dark brown sugar
1 ½ cups white sugar
3 tablespoons honey
1 cup whole milk
1 ½ cups pecans
1 teaspoon dark rum

1. Combine brown and white sugar, honey and milk in a 2-quart saucepan.
2. Cook mixture over a medium heat until it comes to a boil. Reduce heat and cook to a soft stage (225 degrees F).
3. Remove from the heat and let stand 10 minutes, then stir in pecans and rum.
4. Using a teaspoon, drop pecan mixture into small mounds onto wax paper. Allow pralines to dry until firm.
5. Peel from paper and store in an airtight container. Makes about 3 dozen.

Croquignoles

⅓ cup butter
1 cup sugar
1 teaspoon vanilla
4 eggs
3¾ cups flour
4 teaspoons baking powder
½ teaspoon grated nutmeg
½ teaspoon salt
½ cup light cream
Oil for frying
Maple syrup or powdered sugar

1. In a large bowl, cream together butter, sugar and vanilla.
2. Beat eggs into butter/sugar mixture, one at a time.
3. Mix together flour, baking powder, nutmeg and salt. Slowly add dry ingredients into the butter egg mixture with the cream and mix to form a dough. Chill for about an hour to stiffen dough.
4. Roll out dough on a lightly floured board to about a ¼ inch in thickness.
5. Cut into 6-by-¾-inch strips. Twist each strip three times. Moisten ends with a little water and pinch ends together.
6. Heat 2 inches of oil into a large saucepan over a medium-high heat.
7. Carefully drop croquignoles into hot oil and fry until golden brown. Remove and drain on paper towels.
8. Before serving, drizzle with maple syrup or dust with powdered sugar. Makes about 2 dozen.

Twelfth Night King's Cake

2 cups butter, softened
2 cups brown sugar
8 large eggs
3¼ cups all-purpose flour, divided
1 teaspoon baking soda
2 teaspoons ground mace

1 teaspoon ground cinnamon
2 ounces finely chopped or ground almonds or pecans
1 large, dry bean
1 ½ cups apricot jam
Toasted sliced almonds or pecans

1. Beat butter at medium speed with an electric mixer until creamy, then gradually add brown sugar.
2. Add eggs, one at a time, beating after each addition.
3. Combine 3 cups flour, baking soda and spices. Gradually blend into butter mixture.
4. Combine remaining ¼ cup flour with almonds; fold into batter.
5. Spoon batter into 2 buttered and parchment-lined 10-inch round cake pans or a 9x13-inch pan.
6. Drop the bean in the batter in a place you will remember.
7. Heat oven to 350 degrees F and bake cake for 30 to 35 minutes or until cakes tests done when a wooden pick inserted in center comes out clean.
8. Remove cake from oven, place on a wire rack to cool for 10 minutes.
9. Remove from pans and continue to cool completely.
10. To finish cake, heat jam in a saucepan until it becomes spreadable. Spread between cake layers or over the top.
11. Garnish cake top with toasted almonds or pecans. Makes 12 servings.

SERVING THE CAKE TO FIND A KING: When selecting a king or queen, cut cake into equal slices. Serve the slices to your guests, instructing them to look for the bean. Following tradition, the man who finds the bean becomes king of the ball, and he has the privilege of choosing a queen.

Chapter 2
EXPANDING THE MISSOURI TABLE

During Missouri's great migration west, provisions and food options depended on where you were going and who you were. From the enslaved who were brought to the Missouri Delta to the immigrants on the western trails and the social elite traveling upriver aboard steamboats, food availability and accessibility defined one's status and quality of life, and this was reflected by what was on your plate.

Southeast Missouri

When Napoleon sold Upper Louisiana to Thomas Jefferson, Missouri had already earned a reputation for setting a fine table, offering a sophisticated cuisine influenced by the French, Spanish, African and Native American cultures. These culinary influences and traditions continued to add diversity to the Missouri table with each migration, which continued under Spain's brief possession.

Before Spain returned Missouri to France, it launched a plan to bolster the population, offering free land, no taxes and religious freedom to settlers—a plum deal that was appealing to slaveholders affected by the 1787 Northwest Ordinance prohibiting enslavement north of the Ohio River. Many of these slaveholders were attracted to the Missouri Delta, located in the Bootheel, an area surrounding New Madrid where the land was ideal for cotton, hemp and rice. William Hunter was one such planter and businessman who came

White Haven's basement kitchen, where Mary Robinson and other enslaved workers cooked meals during winter to provide heat to the main floor of the house. *Ulysses S. Grant National Historic Site Photo Collection.*

to Missouri. His holdings included a mercantile store, fifteen thousand acres that stretched into four states and thirty-six slaves. His palatial home, the Hunter-Dawson House, was built in New Madrid and is one of two surviving plantation homes preserved as a National Historic Site in Missouri.

While the Hunter-Dawson House has a well-appointed dining room, little is known about the food Hunter ate, let alone the diet of his enslaved people. Beyond general ration lists, slaves were generally allowed to supplement what they were given by gardening, hunting and fishing. In an effort to learn about their lives, which included the foodways of the enslaved, the Federal Writers' Project of the Works Progress Administration recorded the memoirs of former Missouri slaves from 1936 to 1938. These interviews, now housed at the Missouri State Archives, recounted their experiences, plantation lives and food memories.

Among those interviewed was Fil Hancock, a former slave whose grandmother was, in his words, a cook for the White folks. During his interview, Hancock spoke of his meals taken in the slave cabins: "[S]alt meat, cabbage, taters, and shortin' bread three times a day. We had plenty of vegetables we raised ourselves. Once a week we had hot biscuits."

Harry Johnson spoke fondly of the corn dodgers (water cornbread), calling them "awful nice with plenty of butter." Another former slave, Dave Harper of Montgomery County—located in a part of Missouri known as Little Dixie, which stretched along the Missouri River—recounted a sorrowful food memory:

> *De next morning after he bought me, de boss carried me to de old woman and told her to take care of me. Dat morning de kettle was full of spareribs and de people fished dem out with sticks. I didn't see no knives or forks. When dey asked me why I didn't get something to eat, I asked 'bout de forks and a table where I could eat. De overseer just cried.*

White Haven, preserved as the Ulysses S. Grant National Historic Site, is the 850-acre plantation of Frederick Dent, Grant's father-in-law. White Haven resembles more of a farm than what most people envision as a plantation. While serving at Jefferson Barracks, the military post located south of St. Louis City, Grant came to White Haven for a visit on the invitation of his former West Point roommate, Frederick Dent. During Grant's second visit, he met Dent's daughter Julia, and four years later the couple were married. In order to be with Julia and his children, he resigned his army commission in 1854 and returned to White Haven to try his hand as a farmer. He worked side by side in the fields with the enslaved, tending row and cash crops, livestock and poultry.

In a letter to his father dated December 28, 1856, written asking for a $500 loan to help fund farm expenses, Grant outlined his intentions for the upcoming growing season: to plant twenty acres of Irish potatoes, five acres each of sweet potatoes and early corn, in addition to five or six acres of cabbage, beets, cucumber pickles and melons, with a goal to keep a wagon going to market daily.

As recorded in the 1850 Agricultural Census of Carondelet County, White Haven's profitable crops included corn, oats, wheat and hay. Chickens were not counted in the census, although this doesn't lessen their importance. Chickens were valuable for their meat, eggs and feathers. Dent's enslaved cook, Mary Robinson, spoke of catching chickens for what she needed for whatever dish she planned for the Dents' table.

Popular chicken dishes of the time ranged from salmagundi, a forerunner to the chef salad; brown chicken fricassee; and chicken pie, a dish southerners

The majority of Missouri's plantations resembled farms, as illustrated in this 1913 photograph of White Haven, now preserved as the Ulysses S. Grant NHS. *Ulysses S. Grant National Historic Site Photo Collection.*

Maryland biscuits, beaten with a mallet to help them rise, as baked by White Haven enslaved cook Mary Robinson, were a favorite of Julia Dent Grant. *Suzanne Corbett.*

preferred for their Thanksgiving table. Turkey for Thanksgiving was pushed as the centerpiece for the holiday table by Sarah Hale, editor of *Godey's Lady's Book*, a northern publication, which made turkey too Yankee-fied for the southern table.

The Dents kept a good table, reflecting their southern tradition, which was maintained by Mary Robinson's superior culinary skills. Julia spoke fondly of Mary's culinary skills in her personal memoirs:

> *Mammy, Black Mary, was an artist. Such loaves of beautiful snowy cake, such plates full of delicious Maryland biscuit, such exquisite custards and puddings, such omelets, gumbo soup, and fritters—these were mammy's specialty.*

Northeast to Central

By 1800, the English and Scotch-Irish, along with their enslaved African Americans, had arrived from Kentucky, Tennessee, Virginia and Illinois. With them they brought a new cooking skill: they were experts at curing and smoking hams. Hams required more than just know-how—they need the right climate. Missouri was perfect because it shared the same climate conditions as Kentucky, Tennessee, Virginia and Illinois. To successfully cure and smoke hams, you need moderate winters that aren't too cold and summers that aren't too hot. Missouri became and remains one of the few states included the American Ham Belt.

To make a good ham, beside climate, you have to have salt. Salt is vital for both survival and food preservation. Missouri has been blessed with an abundance via its saline springs found throughout the state. Among Missouri's first American settlers who took advantage of harvesting salt from the saline springs was Daniel Boone and his sons.

Boone, who came to Missouri to take advantage of Spain's generous offer of free land, settled in the Femme Osage River Valley near Saline Springs. These springs are west of St. Charles and off the trail Boone blazed that became known as Boone's Lick, named for the springs found along the trail. Boone's sons operated one of the state's most profitable commercial saltworks at the springs, producing thirty bushels of salt per day; the salt was shipped downriver via keelboat to St. Charles and then down on the Mississippi to St. Louis.

A bushel of salt weighs about fifty pounds. Lewis and Clark took three bushels among the provisions on their journey, but it wasn't enough. Before heading back to Missouri from their winter quarters at Fort Clatsop, men from their Corps of Discovery had to harvest salt from seawater.

Besides salt, the Corps of Discovery's keelboat was packed with seven tons of provisions. Some of those food supplies included coffee, flour, salt pork, corn, sugar, lard, dried beans and 193 pounds of portable soup. Portable soup was a base made by boiling down bone broth to the point that it thickens into a gelatinous paste; it was then dried and cut into pieces. Sort of like a forerunner to bouillon cubes, it was taken as a survival food, intended for use when food supplies ran thin or when hunting was bad. When hunting was good, Lewis and Clark's men ate well. Clark wrote in his journal, dated July 13, 1805, "We eat an immensity of meat; it requires 4 deer, or an elk and a deer, or one buffalo to supply us plentifully 24 hours."

Another journal entry noted a makeshift recipe used during a food shortage: a mixture of flour and foraged berries that produced something similar to a cobbler. Clark reported how his hungry men proclaimed that it was the best thing they had eaten in a long time.

SOUTHWEST BY NORTHWEST

Six years after Lewis and Clark returned, Missouri became a state. The same year, William Becknell, a trader who operated a ferry on the Missouri River between Arrow Rock and Franklin, organized the first trading caravan to Santa Fe. Conveniently, Becknell made the Franklin and Arrow Rock trailheads—an added boost to his ferry business.

When the Santa Fe Trail opened, it ignited trade, western migration and a food exchange, primarily bringing together Spanish cattle, Mexican red beans and chiles—all ingredients used in chile con carne, another food addition to Missouri whose Americanized versions (with and without beans) fed cattle drovers pushing herds to Kansas City. Variations of the dish swapped out whatever meat could be found along the trail. The same substitution was made for beef and beans, another recipe that filled the cookpots of settlers who left on the Oregon and California Trails from the Queen City of the Trails, Independence; the recipe was just as tasty made with buffalo, squirrel or rabbit.

CIVILIZED MEALS

Travelers arriving by wagon or steamboat often yearned for one last civilized meal and a night's lodging before heading west. To satisfy the hungry, tavern inns sprang up along the routes, serving what often was the last civilized meal—a meal served on a table set with all the accoutrements (flatware and china) that the inn could afford. Arrow Rock's J. Huston Tavern was counted among the best stops.

Joseph Huston quickly realized that good money could be made by opening his home for lodging and meals. Huston opened his tavern in 1834, charging two bits (twenty-five cents) for a meal and a night's lodging. If you wanted only the meal, it cost twelve and a half cents. According to Arrow Rock foodways interpreters, meals served were generally stews or soups—the fast food of their day. More elaborate meals such as fried chicken, served with sides and pie, would not have been on the daily menu

Arrow Rock's J. Huston Tavern was one of the last stops where a civilized meal could be bought (for twelve and a half cents) before heading west. *Suzanne Corbett.*

but rather were offered on select days. Fried chicken is now served daily at the Arrow Rock Tavern, which hasn't stopped serving since it was opened, making Arrow Rock Tavern the oldest continuously operating restaurant west of the Mississippi River.

Joseph Robidoux, an accomplished trader and founder of St. Joseph, also knew how to turn a profit accommodating travelers, especially those arriving by steamboat. He opened what became Robidoux Row, an apartment/hotel that rented rooms outfitted with cookpots and utensils. Doorways were built high enough off the ground for a wagon to easily pull up to and unload. Rent was one dollar a day for those waiting their turn on the ferry to cross the river. However, Robidoux allowed some guests to stay for free, provided they were building a house in town on the land he had sold them.

Steamboat Bill of Fare and Culinary Cargo

What's your pleasure? Boiled turkey, chicken fricassee, stewed duck or perhaps something simple like green turtle soup, pork and beans or apple pie. This is a sampling of the dozens of selections for first-class passengers on the 1847 bill of fare for the steamboat *Missouri*. These meals were often included with the price of the ticket for those upper-deck passengers. Steerage passengers were out of luck; if they didn't bring their own food or have money to purchase food on board, they went hungry—a painful contrast of the haves and have-nots of the era. Nonetheless, the steamboat's upper-deck society had plenty, indulging in dishes prepared with the finest ingredients—culinary luxuries of the day like celery and libations such as French Champagne, brandies and Kentucky bourbon. The food and drinks were served by African Americans in lavishly appointed dining salons like those made famous by the *J.M. White* steamboat, whose opulent salon was re-created for the *American Queen* steamboat in the 1990s.

Examples of some of those foods—which could have been enjoyed at the table or picked up at the general store—were found in 1988 on what proved the ultimate time capsule: the steamboat *Arabia*. On September 5, 1856, the *Arabia* hit a snag in the Missouri River just south of Kansas City and sank with 220 tons of cargo. Millions of items were found. Items related to the table included 807 knives, 676 forks, 665 spoons, 27 coffeepots, china, glassware and a collection of kitchenware ranging from baking pans and rolling pins to coffee mills and syrup mugs. Each represented the sellable items that ladies found important to setting a nice table.

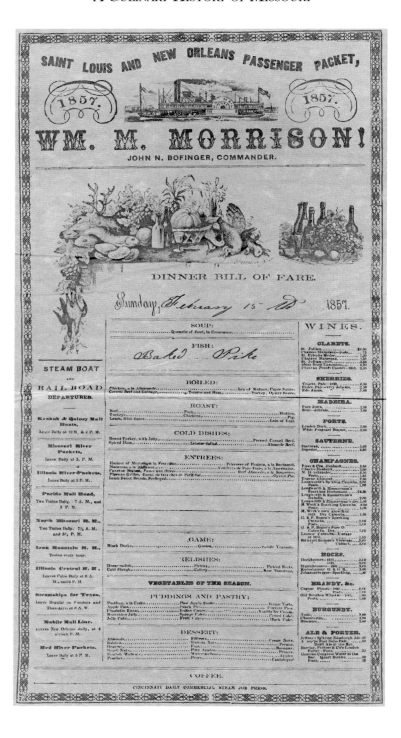

Opposite: The February 15, 1857 dinner bill of fare offered to passengers aboard the *Wm. M. Morrison* steamboat. *Herman T. Pott National Inland Waterways Library at University of Missouri–St. Louis.*

Above: Pickles, oysters, cherries and Champagne—a portion of the food-related cargo recovered from the steamboat *Arabia*, which sank in the Missouri River. *Visit KC.*

The most exciting finds were the foods—canned oysters, pickles, bottled cherries and rhubarb for pies, French Champagne and sweet pickles, many of which were still edible and drinkable. These foods illustrated the variety of commercially made products marketed to enhance the menu and make frontier life more palatable.

NORTHWEST MISSOURI

Westward trails brought more than just people to Independence, Kansas City and St. Joseph. They brought wheat and cattle, commodities that spurred the meatpacking, milling and commercial baking industries. This boom was made possible due to the Kansas Pacific Railroad and the Missouri Pacific Railroad, which saw the opportunities and established hubs in Kansas City after the Civil War.

The Kansas City Stockyards, which opened on the Kansas side of the Missouri River in 1871, jumped the river to the Missouri side in 1875 in order to accommodate the estimated 400,000 steers brought by cattlemen for processing and shipping. Hundreds of thousands of cattle were shipped live to Chicago's Union Stockyards and to St. Louis's stockyards for processing. These locations had companies that supplied canned beef and pork to the government during the Civil War and then decided to expand operations into Kansas City and St. Joseph. Armour, Star and Swift were among the first to open large-scale meat processing plants west of the Mississippi.

Cattle wasn't the only moneymaker crossing the Kansas-Missouri border. Turkey Red wheat, a hard winter variety, was brought by Russian immigrants to the area in the 1870s. The wheat flourished in the prairie climate, producing bumper crops.

Turkey Red revitalized milling operations. One of the more famous area flour mills was the Waggoner & Gates Milling Company. The company began when Peter Waggoner bought the city's old mill; with his partner George Gates, they rebuilt the mill and ditched the millstones, opting instead for the latest milling technology, steel rollers, which expelled the bran and germ, yielding a light white flour they packaged as "Queen of the

The Kansas City Stockyards, which began in Kansas before stretching into Missouri, covering fifty-five acres. In its heyday, it accommodated more than 2.5 million steers annually. *Visit KC.*

Pantry Flour." It was the preferred flour brand used at the White House during the Truman administration. The president happily promoted the company from his hometown, which delighted his wife, Bess, as she was the granddaughter of Gates.

By the time the Pearl Milling Company began operations a few years later in St. Joseph, the flour market was glutted. With demand down, Pearl's owners developed a pancake mix to help pick up sales. The mix was based on their self-rising flour, mixed with the addition of a little corn flour. The mix was sold in paper bags as Pearl Milling Company Self-Rising Pancake Flour. The following year, Pearl renamed the brand Aunt Jemima Pancake Mix.

The Pearl Milling Company, being undercapitalized, was sold two years later to the Davis Milling Company. Another St. Joseph company, Davis Milling refined the recipe further by adding rice flour and powdered milk, a combination that made Aunt Jemima the first all-in-one pancake mix, whose directions read "Just add water."

In 1926, Davis Milling sold to Quaker Oaks, which was acquired by PepsiCo in 2001. PepsiCo announced in 2021 that in an effort to make positive progress for racial equality, the Aunt Jemima brand would be retired. In its place, it returned to the product's original name, Pearl Milling Company Pancake Mix.

Missouri commercial bakers' good fortunes continued with Sunshine Biscuits and Saltine Crackers, owned by Keebler and Nabisco, respectively. Each company baked similar yet distinctive crackers and cookies. F.L. Sommer & Company, founded in St. Joseph in 1876, upgraded the soda cracker by adding yeast with the baking soda to the dough. The combination created a tender, crisper cracker—nothing like tooth-breaking hardtack, made with flour, water and salt. Sommer named his cracker Premium Soda Crackers, which he later changed to Saltines.

The Kansas City–based Loose-Wiles Biscuit Company, another late nineteenth-century cracker baker, built a reputation on Uneeda Crackers, another crisp, all-purpose cracker. The company promoted its crackers as an ingredient that could be used in other recipes, including Mock Apple Pie, aka Cracker Pie, a recipe Sunshine resurrected during the 1930s Great Depression using its Ritz Crackers. However, Cracker Pie has been around since the 1830s—this fact was also promoted along with the recipe printed on the Saltines box.

CENTRAL MISSOURI

The Missouri River's first one hundred miles, beginning from St. Charles to Hermann, haven't changed much. Rolling hills, terraced vineyards and quaint villages and towns that dot the hillsides would still be recognizable to the Germans who settled the region nearly in the 1830s.

Germans were attracted to the area because of the landscape and climate, which reminded them of the Rhine Valley; this was especially true for the members of the Philadelphia Settlement Society, an organization of German immigrants who bought 11,300 acres in 1837, establishing the city of Hermann. The society sold city lots, called "grape lots," to anyone for fifty dollars, interest free for five years. The catch was you had to plant grapes. The plan worked. More than six hundred grape lots were sold, fostering Hermann's wine industry, which would shock the international wine world when Hermann's Stone Hill Winery won eight of the twelve gold medals awarded during the 1873 Vienna World's Fair.

Stone Hill Winery, established in 1847, was originally named for its founder, Michael Poeschel. Poeschel would partner with John Scherer before selling out to George Stark, who changed the name to Stone Hill. Stark was not related to the Stark brothers, who founded in 1816 the famous Louisiana, Missouri nursery that discovered and developed the Golden Delicious apple. Nonetheless, Stark's management allowed Stone Hill to achieve astronomic success. By the dawn of the twentieth century, Stone Hill had become the largest winery west of the Mississippi, the second largest in the United States and the third largest in the world.

Across and downriver from Hermann is the village of Augusta, which soon saw its wine industry grow as well. Founded as Mount Pleasant in 1836 on land purchased from one of Daniel Boone's followers, by the time it was officially incorporated it had changed its name to Augusta. About the same time, brothers Friedrich and George Muench arrived, establishing Mount Pleasant Winery and naming it in honor of Augusta's previous identity.

Friedrich became a pioneer in the Missouri grape and wine industry, publishing his *Amerikanische Weinbauschule* (which loosely translates to *American Wine School and Grape Culture*). This book influenced Missouri grape growers and vintners, including George Husmann, considered the father of Missouri's grape industry, who took his knowledge to Napa Valley to help establish its vineyards. Mount Peasant also captured its share of international gold medals. Its display during the1904 World's Fair was among the most impressive exhibits of Missouri companies.

Stone Hill Winery's 50th Anniversary Jubilee poster. Stone Hill remains Missouri's oldest, most celebrated winery in the state. *Stone Hill Winery, History Uncorked exhibit, St. Louis Mercantile Library at the University of Missouri–St. Louis.*

All was good in Augusta and Hermann until Prohibition, which saw wineries large and small being forced to uproot vineyards and empty barrels. One small Augusta vineyard winery, owned by Alfred Nahm, was able to stay afloat through Prohibition by selling grapes for religious and medicinal purposes as well as to individuals who by law were allowed to make two hundred gallons of wine annually for personal use. Nahm has the distinction of being the first Missouri winery officially licensed after Prohibition. Unfortunately, the Nahm Winery, which operated adjacent to Centennial Farms, closed shortly after reopening. Nahm was a relative of the Knoernschilds—the family farms the land they have owned since 1854 and operates Centennial Farms, located on the edge of Augusta.

RECIPES

By the time Missouri became a state, more food diversity and dishes were being added to the table—a direct result of the influx of people representing different ethnicities who brought their own unique foods and old country recipes, which were soon Americanized after arrival.

One new skill was another contribution to the cook's repertoire, something that would enhance the Missouri table: many cooks could now read. Cookbooks and "receipts" (recipes) published in popular magazines such as *Godey's Lady's Book* influenced food and tabletop trends. The following recipes reflect a combination of those vintage nineteenth-century recipes, including those interpreted at historic sites throughout Missouri.

Corn Dodgers/Hot Water Cornbread

1 cup cornmeal (white or yellow)
1 teaspoon salt
1 cup boiling water
2 tablespoons melted butter or bacon grease for frying
Butter
Sorghum or maple syrup

1. Place cornmeal in a mixing bowl with salt.
2. Stir in the boiling water and the melted butter.

3. When mixture is cool enough to handle, shape into cakes/patties about a ½-inch thick.
4. Using a cast-iron skillet, pour enough oil or bacon grease to cover the bottom of the skillet.
5. Heat over a medium heat. When oil is hot, fry cornmeal cakes until browned on both sides.
6. Remove corn dodgers and serve with butter and sorghum or maple syrup. Makes 4 servings.

Short'nin Bread

2 cups butter
1 cup brown sugar
4 cups flour
½ teaspoon salt

1. Line a 17x11.5-inch jellyroll pan with parchment or spray with nonstick spray.
2. In a large bowl of a mixer, cream the butter; beat in the sugar until very light and fluffy. Add flour and salt, mixing until smooth.
3. Press the dough evenly onto the prepared pan.
4. Score the dough into squares, eight on the long side of the pan by six on the shorter side.
5. Bake for 25 to 30 minutes or until lightly browned.
6. Remove from oven and immediately cut through the score marks into squares.
7. Cool thoroughly before serving. Makes 48 pieces.

Fried Catfish with Wilted Greens

4 boneless catfish filets
Salt, black pepper and cayenne pepper
1 ½ cups cornmeal
Oil

½ cup finely chopped onion
½ pound greens (sorrel, spinach or turnip greens)
¼ cup vinegar

1. Season fish with salt and pepper and sprinkle with cayenne pepper.
2. Roll fish filets in cornmeal to coat well on both sides. If desired, fish can be dipped in milk or buttermilk before rolling into the cornmeal.
3. Pour a ¼ inch of oil in the bottom of a cast-iron skillet and place over a medium heat.
4. Fry catfish in hot oil until golden brown on each side.
5. Remove fish from skillet and keep warm.
6. Add onions to the now empty skillet and sauté for a minute. Add a tablespoon of oil if pan is dry.
7. Add greens and vinegar and stir until greens have wilted. Season to taste with salt and pepper.
8. Plate catfish with wilted greens and serve. Makes 4 servings.

Brown Fricassee Chicken

1 whole (2½- to 3-pound) chicken, cut into pieces
Flour
Salt and pepper
¼ cup melted butter
2 cups water or chicken broth
2 tablespoons parsley
1 tablespoon fresh thyme
1 medium onion, chopped
2 tablespoons lemon juice
2 tablespoons cornstarch
Parsley sprigs for garnish

1. Dust chicken with flour and season with salt and pepper.
2. Heat butter in a heavy Dutch oven over a medium heat. Sauté chicken in the butter until browned on all sides. Add more melted butter as needed to complete browning.

3. Pour in water and remove from heat. Sprinkle parsley, thyme and onion over chicken; cover and bake at 350 degrees F for 1 hour.
4. Remove cover and continue to bake until chicken is tender. Remove from oven and transfer chicken to a serving platter. Cover chicken with foil and keep warm.
5. Place baking pan on stovetop over a low heat.
6. In a small bowl, mix together lemon juice and cornstarch. Slowly whisk into the pan drippings and cook until sauce thickens.
7. Pour sauce over chicken and serve. Makes 4 to 6 servings.

Maryland Beaten Biscuits

4 cups unbleached flour
1 teaspoon salt
½ cup lard or butter
1 ½ cups water or milk

1. Place flour, salt and lard/butter in a mixing bowl. Cut lard into flour using fingertips until lard is mixed into flour.
2. Mix in a few tablespoons of the water or milk at a time until mixture forms a stiff dough. If dough is too dry, add a little more liquid. If too wet, add a little more flour.
3. Place dough on a worktable that has been lightly floured.
4. Using a mallet or rolling pin beat the dough until it begins to blister. This takes about a half hour.
5. Pat dough out to about an inch in thickness. Cut into rounds and place on a greased or parchment-lined baking sheet.
6. Using a fork, poke a few holes in the top of each biscuit.
7. Bake at 425 degrees F for 20 to 25 minutes or until brown. Makes about 2 dozen biscuits.

1830 Chicken Pie

1 (2½- to 3-pound) chicken
Water
1 or 2 small onions
salt and pepper
3 cups chopped vegetables (a combination of chopped potatoes, carrots and onions)
1 egg, beaten
Poultry gravy or chicken broth
Salt and pepper
1 tablespoon minced chive
1 tablespoon thyme leaves
Pie pastry or biscuit dough
Egg wash (1 egg beaten with 2 tablespoons of water)

1. Place chicken in a large stockpot and cover with water. Add an onion or two and season with salt and pepper.
2. Bring chicken to a boil over a medium-high heat, then reduce and simmer until chicken is fork tender.
3. Remove chicken from broth and allow to cool. Strain and reserve broth.
4. Debone chicken, discarding bones and chicken skin. Chop or shred chicken meat and place in a bowl with vegetables.
5. Mix in egg and enough gravy or reserved broth to bind filling together. Season with salt, pepper and herbs.
6. Place pie pastry into a pie or baking pan; top with chicken filling and cover with another layer of pastry. If using biscuit dough, pour filling into a greased baking pan and drop biscuit dough by the spoonful on top. (Variation: Line pie pan with pastry, add filling and then crumble leftover baked biscuits over top.)
7. Brush top crust with egg wash, which promotes browning.
8. Bake at 450 degrees F for 10 minutes and then reduce heat to 375 degrees. Continue to bake until vegetables are tender and crust is brown. Makes 6 servings.

Country Cured Baked Ham

1 (7- or 8-pound) dry-cured ham
Water
Apple cider
Honey
Seasoned dried breadcrumbs

1. Wash the outside of the ham, using warm water and a vegetable brush to remove any residue or mold that isn't penetrating that may be on the outside surface of the ham. Mold is a normal occurrence from the curing process.
2. Place ham in a large bowl or kettle and cover with cold water. Soak ham for 12 hours and then pour off water and replace with fresh water. Allow to soak for at least another 12 hours or overnight.

To Boil the Ham:
3. Remove ham from the soaking water and place in a large stockpot or roaster fitted with a rack to prevent bottom of ham from scorching. Cut off ham hock if ham is too large to fit into pot.
4. Place on stovetop and cover ham with apple cider.
5. Bring to a boil and then reduce immediately to a simmer. Simmer ham until it becomes fork tender. This will take 4 to 5 hours.
6. Remove ham from simmering liquid and place on a baking rack, skin side up.
7. Carefully cut rind from ham, leaving about a ¼-inch layer of the fat. Discard rind and score ham using a crosshatch design.
8. Brush top of ham with honey, allowing honey to seep down into the scoring.
9. Lightly sprinkle breadcrumbs over ham and bake at 400 degrees F until breadcrumbs are lightly browned, about 15 to 20 minutes.
10. Remove ham from oven and allow to rest for 15 minutes before slicing. Number of servings depends on size of ham. Serving sizes are generally based on 8 ounces.

Voyageur Rendezvous Soup

Recipe from *The Food Journal of Lewis & Clark* by Mary Gunderson

½ cup chopped bacon
1 cup chopped onion
1 to 2 cloves garlic, chopped
1 pound of dry yellow split peas, rinsed
6 cups chicken broth
2 bay leaves
salt and pepper to taste
1 pound smoke ham, cut into chunks
1 or 2 potatoes, peeled and chopped

1. In a large Dutch oven placed over a medium-high heat, sauté bacon for a few minutes.
2. Add onion and garlic and sauté for a few minutes, then add peas and broth.
3. Add in remaining ingredients, reduce heat to low and simmer for 1 hour.
4. Remove bay leaves and discard. Adjust seasoning to taste with salt and pepper. Makes 6 to 8 servings.

Skillet Fried Trout

Salt and pepper
2 whole trout or 4 boneless trout fillets
Flour
4 tablespoons butter
2 slices bacon, thinly sliced
½ cup lemon juice or apple cider vinegar
2 tablespoons green onions

1. Salt and pepper the trout inside and out, then dust with flour.
2. Heat butter and bacon in a large skillet over a medium heat. Sauté for a few minutes to partially cook bacon.
3. Place trout in the skillet and fry until browned on each side. This takes about three to five minutes on each side.

4. Remove trout from skillet, place on serving place and cover to keep warm.
5. Add lemon juice and green onions to the skillet to deglaze pan. Stir, scraping the bottom of the pan to make a light sauce.
6. Pour pan sauce over trout and serve. Makes 4 servings.

Rabbit with White Gravy

1 (1½- pound) rabbit, cut into serving-size pieces
½ cup flour
Oil or bacon drippings
Salt and pepper
1 large onion, chopped
¼ cup water
1 bay leaf
¼ cup vinegar
2 tablespoons flour
1½ cups whole milk

1. Dredge rabbit with flour, shaking off any excess.
2. In a large skillet, add enough oil to cover the bottom of the pan with about a ¼ inch. Heat oil over a medium heat.
3. Add rabbit to skillet and generously season with salt and pepper.
4. When rabbit has browned on each side, add the onion, water, bay leaf and vinegar. Cover and simmer until rabbit is tender, about 60 minutes.
5. Remove rabbit from the skillet, place on a platter and cover to keep warm while finishing sauce.
6. To make gravy, whisk the flour into the pan drippings and cook for about a minute. Slowly whisk in milk. Cook gravy until it thickens. Season to taste with salt, pepper and a little more vinegar if desired.
7. Pour gravy over rabbit and serve. Makes 4 servings.

Tavern Fried Chicken

1 (2½-pound) chicken
8 cups water
1 tablespoon salt
4 cups buttermilk
1 cup flour
½ cup white cornmeal
Salt and pepper to taste
1 teaspoon flour
Lard or oil

1. Rinse chicken and cut up into serving pieces.
2. Mix water and salt together in a bowl large. Add chicken, cover and refrigerate overnight.
3. Remove chicken from brine and place in a clean bowl. Cover chicken with buttermilk, refrigerate and marinate for at least 4 hours.
4. Mix flour and cornmeal together in a bowl. Season flour mixture to taste with salt and pepper.
5. Remove chicken from buttermilk, shaking off excess, and then dredge in seasoned flour mix. Place on a wire rack to dry.
6. Heat a skillet over a medium heat. Add enough lard or oil to cover bottom of skillet by a ½ inch.
7. Add chicken to skillet in a single layer. Fry until golden brown on each side, 20 to 35 minutes, depending on the size and piece of the chicken. Makes 2 to 4 servings.

Hickory Nut Pie

1 cup sugar
2 tablespoons cornstarch
¼ teaspoon salt
1 cup water
½ cup molasses
4 eggs, slightly beaten
1 teaspoon vanilla

1 cup coarsely broken hickory nuts
1 unbaked pastry shell

1. In a saucepan, combine sugar, cornstarch and salt. Whisk in water and molasses.
2. Place over medium heat and stir until mixture thickens.
3. Place eggs in a large bowl. Slowly whisk in hot syrup mixture at little at a time to prevent eggs from cooking.
4. Add vanilla and the hickory nuts and pour into an unbaked pastry shell.
5. Bake at 350 degrees F for 45 minutes or until the filling is set. Test by inserting a knife tip in the center of pie; if it comes out clean, it's done.
6. Remove and cool on a rack. Makes one pie, yielding 6 to 8 servings.

Quick Pickles

1 ½ cups small heirloom tomatoes or cherry tomatoes
1 medium cucumber, sliced into bite-size pieces
1 cup chopped green bell pepper
4 green onions, chopped
¼ cup chopped parsley
1 tablespoon sugar
1 teaspoon salt
1 teaspoon black pepper
¾ cup cider vinegar

1. In a large bowl, combine tomatoes, cucumber, green pepper, onions and parsley.
2. In a small bowl, mix together sugar, salt, pepper and vinegar.
3. Pour over vegetables, adding more vinegar if needed to cover vegetables.
4. Refrigerate and marinate for at least 4 hours before serving. Makes 6 to 8 servings.

Beef Olives

6 ¼-inch-thick slices beef round
Salt and pepper to taste
1 ½ cups dry plain breadcrumbs
2 thick slices smoked bacon, finely chopped
1 cup minced white onion
1 tablespoon fresh marjoram
1 egg
Wine or milk
Flour
2 tablespoons butter or lard
Water or beef stock
Horseradish

1. Place beef slices on a work surface and sprinkle with salt and pepper.
2. In a large mixing bowl, combine breadcrumbs, bacon, onion, salt, pepper, marjoram and the egg. Add enough wine or milk to just moisten the breadcrumb mixture.
3. Divide dressing among the veal slices and roll up, fastening shut with skewers or wooden picks.
4. Dust with flour and season with salt and pepper.
5. Heat butter or lard in a skillet and quickly sear beef olives on all sides. This takes only a few minutes.
6. Place beef olives in a buttered baking pan. Add enough water or stock to just cover the bottom of the pan.
7. Cover and bake at 400 degrees for 45 minutes, or until beef olives are tender. Remove cover during last 10 minutes of baking to promote browning.
8. Remove from oven and carefully remove picks or skewers. Place beef olives on a serving platter.
9. Serve with horseradish and, if desired, a gravy made from the pan drippings. To make the gravy, whisk a cup of stock or wine with a flour slurry (2 tablespoons flour mixed with ¼ cup water) into pan drippings and cook until it thickens. Makes 6 servings.

Kettle Cooked Beef

¼ cup oil
2½- to 3-pound beef roast (chuck or bottom round)
Flour
Salt and pepper to taste
2 large onions, sliced
6 carrots, cut into 1-inch pieces
½ cup water

1. In a large Dutch oven, heat oil over a medium-high heat.
2. Dust beef roast with flour and place in Dutch oven to sear.
3. Season beef with salt and pepper and sear until browned on all sides.
4. Reduce heat to low and add onions, carrots and water.
5. Cover and simmer for 2 to 2½ hours, or until beef is fork tender. If beef becomes too dry during simmering, add a little water to prevent beef from sticking and burning.
6. Remove beef and vegetables from Dutch oven. Gently shred beef or, if preferred, cut into slices. Plate with vegetables. Makes 8 to 10 servings.

Cowboy Beef and Beans

1 pound dried pinto beans
6 cups water
Oil or bacon drippings
2½ pounds beef chuck, cut into bite-size pieces
½ cup flour
Salt and pepper to taste
2 cups thinly sliced onions
2 cups tomato juice
¼ cup molasses
½ cup chopped mild green or hot red peppers
1 teaspoon dry mustard

1. Rinse the beans in cold water and place in a large saucepan with the 6 cups of fresh water.

61

2. Bring beans to a boil, turn off heat and let stand for 1 hour.
3. Add enough oil or bacon drippings to just cover the bottom of a Dutch oven, then heat over a medium-high heat.
4. Dust beef with flour and season with salt and pepper. Place beef in Dutch oven and brown on all sides.
5. Add the soaked beans (including the water that hasn't been absorbed into the beans), onions, tomato juice, molasses, green or hot red peppers, salt and pepper and dry mustard.
6. Cover and simmer on the stovetop for 1½ hours, until beef is fork tender. If beef and beans become too dry during cooking, add a little water. Serve with Fried Soda Biscuits. Makes 6 to 8 servings.

Fried Soda Biscuits

2 cups flour
½ teaspoon salt
1 teaspoon baking soda
¼ cup lard or shortening
¾ cup buttermilk
Oil or lard for frying
Honey or molasses

1. Combine flour, salt and baking soda in a mixing bowl, then cut lard into flour mixture.
2. Stir in buttermilk and gently knead into a ball.
3. Pinch off small pieces of dough and roll into balls.
4. In a large skillet, heat enough oil to cover biscuits.
5. Slightly flatten dough balls and slide biscuits into the hot oil (375 degrees F). Fry until golden brown on both sides. Remove and drain on paper towels or a wire rack.
6. Serve hot with honey or molasses. Makes about a dozen biscuits.

Saltine Cracker Pie

1 teaspoon butter
14 saltine crackers
1 cup pecans
1 teaspoon baking powder
3 egg whites
1 cup sugar
1 teaspoon vanilla

1. Heat oven to 350 degrees F and butter a 9-inch pie pan.
2. Crumble crackers into a mixing bowl; add pecans and baking powder.
3. Beat egg whites until stiff, then slowly beat in sugar and vanilla.
4. Fold egg whites into cracker mixture. Pour into the buttered pie pan.
5. Bake for 25 to 30 minutes, or until pie is golden brown and top is crusty.
6. Remove from oven and cool completely. Makes 1 pie.

Queen of the Pantry Pound Cake
Courtesy National Archives Foundation

1 pound sugar (2 cups)
1 pound butter (2 cups), softened to room temperature
9 eggs, separated
1 pound cake flour (4½ cups)
1 teaspoon vanilla

1. Combine sugar and butter in a large mixing bowl; mix until fluffy.
2. Beat egg yolks until frothy, then add to butter/sugar mixture.
3. Mix in flour gradually, then add vanilla.
4. Beat egg whites until stiff. Fold into batter mixture.
5. Pour batter into a greased and floured tube cake pan.
6. Bake at 325 degrees F for 1 hour, or until cake tests done. Makes 1 cake, serving 10 to 12 slices.

Chapter 3

GILDED TABLES TO FLAVORFUL FAIRS

*Part of the secret of the success in life is to eat what you like
and let the food fight it out inside.*
—Mark Twain

Conspicuous consumption literally ruled the dining table during America's Gilded Age, an era generally defined as spanning the post–Civil War period to World War I, when the table and menu revealed one's success. Your status, wealth and prestige were mirrored in your plate because what you ate and how and where you dined revealed who you were.

Extravagant tables were glorified in spite of the fact that a good deal of Missourians sustained themselves on meager meals eaten from tables set with mismatched dishes. Yet this was an era when the middle class was emerging; its increased financial stability allowed for fancier foods and tabletops. More could afford the indulgence of dining out, enjoying luxurious, multi-course menus designed to impress, emulating experiences found inside plush dining cars, hotels and the mansions of the high society.

As the Gilded Age waned, Missouri launched its state fair in 1901 to celebrate its agricultural achievements through exhibits and competitions, including culinary competitions designed to give the ladies a platform to exhibit their homespun baking and canning skills. Exhibiting Missouri's best was magnified on an international scale for seven months in 1904 during the Louisiana Purchase Exposition, better known as the St. Louis World's Fair. This event forever changed not only the Missouri table but also how the rest of the country would eat.

NORTHEAST TO NORTHWEST: DINING WITH THE RAILROAD

Railroads were always about the hookup—hooking up any place track could be laid for transporting people and servicing a potential demand for goods to an ever-growing market. It proved the one-two punch that effectively killed off the steamboats, which in turn changed the American table.

Railroads were able to cut days, sometimes weeks, off transportation, making more food accessible and affordable. What the railroads achieved for the meat industry would be repeated for fresh produce and fruits from places like the Ozarks, which had seen regional limitations.

Railroads would soon make beer barons such as Adolphus Busch richer, as they realized that the railroad was key to distribution and the company's future success. In 1887, Busch established the Manufacturers Railway, a short line that hooked onto the Terminal Railroad's tracks. It was a stroke of marketing genius, carrying beer across the Mississippi and into eastern markets.

Wabash passengers traveling from St. Louis to Kansas City expected to dine in style, as the table place setting illustrates. *Suzanne Corbett.*

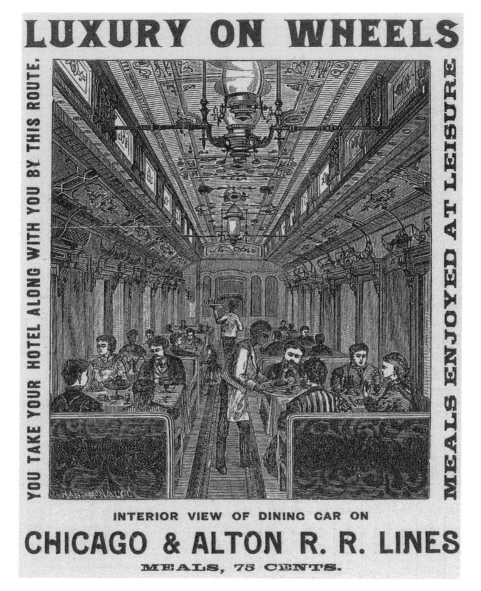

An 1880s print advertisement featuring a Pullman dining car and the meal service on the Chicago & Alton Railroad, whose lines serviced Missouri destinations. *Chicago & Alton Railroad Collection.*

As the railroad's freight inventory increased, so did its passenger service. These passengers brought their luggage along with their appetites, and they would need more than the questionable greasy spoons that lined the tracks near water stops. It didn't take long for the railroads to figure out that food service was a customer priority.

A few railroads rolled out what were called buffet cars and refreshment cars, but those failed. George Pullman figured it out with the unveiling of his hotel car in 1868. These plush cars were outfitted with fine china and crystal—perhaps not the best choice to use on moving trains. However, the idea was solid, and after a few modifications, the dining car was born. The Missouri Pacific, whose tracks reached most of Missouri, made its dining car service famous, offering menu selections as Crab Louis and Chicken à la King, and for heartier appetites, there was roast turkey, broiled strip steaks and Swiss Steak Jardinière. Everything was plated on heavier, logoed china, with flatware and linens, including the tiny milk bottles that accompanied the coffee service and sported the MoPac logo along with the dairy's name. It was a marketing triumph, conveying the idea that MoPac provided the freshest and best food found along the line.

Off the train and back at the station, another food renaissance was happening with dining at St. Louis Union Station and Kansas City's Union Station, the last of the Gilded Age's palatial train stations. Included among the sites were Harvey House restaurants. Fred Harvey is credited with creating the first restaurant chain, a career he first considered as a Missourian. He opened his first restaurant in 1855 in St. Louis, but it didn't last—a casualty of the Civil War and a bad partnership. However, lessons were learned that he would use to build his restaurant empire.

Harvey returned to St. Louis in 1894 to open another of his famous Harvey House restaurants. The brand would expand into Kansas City's Union Station after it opened in 1914, after Harvey's death. Both the Kansas City and St. Louis locations became the training grounds for Harvey's most lasting imprint on American dining: the Harvey Girl—the ultimate waitress who provided effective and pleasant service.

Northeast: Dining with Savoir Faire

An engraved dinner invitation was society's most valued commodity. Such invitations for an evening of dining and polite conversation were a sign that you had socially arrived. Mark Twain, who coined the name Gilded

Age, embraced such luxurious dining occasions yet still mocked the social protocols. But it didn't matter. He reveled in such glorious affairs as those hosted for him by John Garth and John Cruikshank, owners of Woodside and Rockcliffe, respectively—two of Hannibal's Gilded Age mansions. Each has its own Twain connection. Each is preserved and operated today as a bed-and-breakfast and special event venue.

When Twain visited Hannibal in 1882 and 1902, he stayed and dined at Garth Woodside Mansion. John Garth was a childhood friend of Twain's, and they remained friends throughout their lives. Cruikshank was Hannibal's lumber baron, and his only connection to Twain was to host his 1902 farewell reception staged at his home, Rockcliffe. An estimated three hundred guests were entertained by Twain's musings from the mansion's ornate grand staircase.

Rockcliffe Mansion and Garth Woodside Mansion are both included in the National Register of Historic Places. Guests have the opportunity to stand on Rockcliffe's staircase where Twain stood or sleep in his bedroom at Woodside. Each provides an elegant breakfast served in a style that Twain would have approved. However, consider that Twain's life itself was a contradiction—he embraced his meager rural beginnings and his Gilded Age excesses, and he would have enjoyed a fried pork tenderloin sandwich lunch, Hannibal's signature plate, served at the vintage 1940s Mark Twain Dinette, located across the street and down the block from his childhood home.

There isn't any record that Mark Twain visited or dined at the home of Robert Campbell. Just as well—he may not have been welcomed. After all, while working as riverboat pilot on one of the steamboats Campbell owned, Twain ran it aground. But perhaps he would have been welcomed after all, as there were many other luminaries visiting St. Louis who were favored with an invitation to dine with Virginia and Robert Campbell.

Virginia Campbell, renowned nineteenth-century St. Louis society matriarch whose dinner parties were covered by the day's press, was described as a hostess with savoir faire. She hosted the leaders of the day, including President Ulysses S. Grant, serving twelve-course dinners, which were often supplemented by the culinary expertise of the city's most opulent hotel, the Southern Hotel, also owned by Robert Campbell.

The menu always reflected the importance of the guest of honor and flaunted the wealth of its provider. Since the Campbells had plenty, plenty was expected on their table. One could always expect an oyster dish, an elegant entrée such as Beef Chasseur and spectacular desserts like Charlotte

The Campbells' gilded table re-creates the 1870s dining style, which was used to wine and dine luminaries of the age, including President U.S. Grant. *Jim Corbett III, Campbell House Museum.*

Russe, the trendy favorite of the day. All were served with wines and the mid-meal aperitif, Roman Punch, a Champagne, citrus juice and simple syrup mixture that is frozen to create a slushy-like consistency.

The Campbells' butler's pantry still holds a collection of silver and the Campbells' Old Paris china, which originally numbered over three hundred pieces; it was reported to have been bought especially for a dinner party planned for then newly elected president Ulysses S. Grant, a friend of the Campbells. This collection mostly remains intact and on display as part of the Campbell House Museum, where its dining table is always set for dinner.

NORTHWEST: DINNER IS SERVED

With one of the highest per-capita incomes in the country, St. Joseph had its share of millionaires. Each one constructed a Gilded Age mansion with dining rooms made to impress, appointed with polished hand-carved wood furnishings, gilded cornices, stained glass and imported tile floors. Topping the list of over-the-top St. Joseph's palaces is the Shakespeare Chateau. This majestic, French-inspired stone chateau was built in 1885 by self-

Above: Place settings evolved to accommodate à la Russe dining, which is the dining style still offered at the J C Wyatt mansion in St. Joseph. *J C Wyatt House.*

Left: Lemon curd and scones, a turn-of-the-century menu must, served at Missouri's finest hotels and mansions, as at the Shakespeare Chateau in St. Joseph. *Shakespeare Chateau.*

made millionaire Nathen Ogden; it was located on Hill Street, better known as "Millionaire's Row."

Shakespeare Chateau, which gets its name from the hand-carved Shakespeare bust incorporated into a parlor mantel, is owned by Isobel McGowan. McGowan restored the chateau, operating it as a bed-and-breakfast and event space and offering tables for four or more for dining experiences fit for a millionaire. They serve multi-course menus in Victorian style. Breakfasts are a little more low-key yet elegant nonetheless, often including fresh lemon curd and scones.

A stone's throw away from Millionaire's Row is the Richardsonian Romanesque–style mansion, the J C Wyatt House. St. Joseph's other Gilded Age dining venue, dating to 1891, was built by John Cavan Wyatt, who made his fortune in the dry goods trade. After the structure fell into disrepair, Jim Pallone and Jeff Keyasko rescued and restored it, returning the house to its glory days of elegant living and, of course, fine dining. Its guests party like it's 1891, stepping back in time to *dine*, not just eat. And there is a difference.

The J C Wyatt's extraordinary, indulgent dining experience begins with the tablescape. The table is set with rare silver serving pieces, flatware, etched crystal stemware and vintage china, befitting its chef-driven menu, which is exactly the way dinners were designed when these million-dollar mansions thrived.

MISSOURI'S GOVERNOR'S MANSION

Dining in Missouri's people's house, the Governor's Mansion, has always required an invitation—one that recipients have valued since 1872, when then governor B. Gratz Brown and his family moved into the current mansion. The fourteen-foot mahogany dining table, which became the centerpiece of the mansion's dining room, is counted among the mansion's oldest furnishings. The handcrafted 1825 table didn't arrive until the 1980s, a purchase of the Bond administration. The Bond table complements the Edwards sideboard, which has been in service since the Edwards administration (1844–48); one of the sideboard's intriguing features are the circular lidded areas located on both sides of the piece, which are interpreted as plate warmers.

Anyone dining or touring the dining room can't overlook the mansion's magnificent silver service from the USS *Missouri*. Upholding the tradition of silver gifted to the ship that carries a state's name, the punch bowl was the first silver piece originally gifted by Missouri to the navy in 1903 for use on the USS *Missouri* (BB-11), the second naval vessel to hold the name. The first was a side-wheel steam frigate that sank in 1843. The third, USS *Missouri* (BB-63), the "Mighty MO," inherited the punch bowl and was gifted additional silver in the form of eighteen five-piece place settings of silver flatware and service pieces. The Mighty MO, whose history stretches from World War II to the Gulf War, is now a museum at Pearl Harbor. Its silver was returned to Missouri and remains at the Governor's Mansion, except for one place setting, which is on display at the Harry S. Truman Presidential Library and Museum in Independence.

State Fair and World's Fair Fare

The Missouri State Fair is all about the food—a week and half of culinary adoration held each August for Missouri's agricultural products, livestock and the best baked, pickled and canned goods from its cooks. Everything is celebrated with ribbons, cash awards, recognition and bragging rights.

An annual event since 1901, staged on the four-hundred-acre Missouri State Fairgrounds in Sedalia, the fair began as the 1850s State Agricultural Society Fair in Booneville but lasted only a few years. Its resurrection is owed to the Missouri Swine Breeders Association, which brought a resolution to the Missouri General Assembly in 1897 to establish an official state fair. Missouri's horse breeders and poultry producers jumped on the bandwagon, sending their own resolutions with support of Governor Stephens. This was a savvy political move resulting in the creation of and funding for the fair.

When the fair opened in 1901, two-thirds of Missourians lived in rural areas. These days, the stats have reversed, which has made the fair's exhibits change. While cattle, sheep and swine still fill the barns, the breeds have changed. Missouri's cattlemen sixty years ago exhibited mostly Herefords and Angus. Today, there are eight new cattle classes, including the Swiss Simmental and Brangus, a cross between Angus and Brahman. These cattle, unlike their blue-ribbon predecessors, all are leaner, a response driven by consumer preferences. It's also a production choice applied to hogs, which are no longer entered into classes labeled as lard hogs or bacon hogs. Prize-winning porkers today are long and lean.

Trimmer livestock isn't the only change witnessed over the last one hundred years at the fair. Food exhibits and contests have changed. That said, spoiler

Preservation entries on display at the Missouri State Fair, which has been a popular competition since the fair began in 1901. *Missouri State Fair.*

alert, the "how many kernels of corn a hog can eat in a day contest" is gone, along with the pie, watermelon and cracker eating contests. Eating contests have disappeared, perhaps a reflection of twenty-first-century concerns for healthier eating; this perhaps also contributed to the demise of the baking-with-lard pie pastry contest.

Competitions listed in the *Missouri State Fair 2021 Premium Guide,* the publication used to officially enter contests, include a few that reflect current food trends. The 2021 *Premium Guide* lists an Appetizer Dip and Gourmet Mac 'n' Cheese cooking contests. Other contests are sponsored and themed, as with the Missouri Wine and Grape Board's Cooking with Wine Contest and the Midwest Foodways Alliance's Family Heirloom Recipe Competition, a contest targeted at preserving family foodways and culinary history, driven by the interest in discovering one's ancestry.

Food entries, which numbered 1,200 back in the early 1970s, have nearly doubled, making the old Home Economics Building a must stop for anyone hungry to learn what Missouri's blue-ribbon cooks are serving. Surrounded by food displays, concessioners are betting that you will get hungry. As always, they're standing ready with a bevy of choices from funnel cakes, lemonade, corn dogs and the assortment of stuff on a stick. For something a little more substantial, Missouri's beef, pork and wine producers offer alternative venues to eat, rest and relax.

Missouri Wine and Grape Program hosts the Missouri Wine Garden, featuring the year's winning wines and juices. Missouri's Beef House, located in a permanent building across from the Home Economics Building, offers plates and sandwiches featuring its house specialty: ribeye steaks. Missouri's Pork Producers offers two dining options: the Pork Stop, a walk-up window for pork burgers, and an air-conditioned dining hall with tables to relax and linger over chops, ribs, pulled pork and BLTs.

THE FAIR, THE FOOD AND THE HILL

We know the list: hot dogs, iced tea, hamburgers and the ice cream cone—foods whose popularity skyrocketed during the 1904 St. Louis World's Fair. It's no wonder why so many proselytized their inventions at the fair. But these foods, as well as the club sandwich, were not developed at the 1904 world's fair, officially named the Louisiana Purchase Exposition.

St. Louis can claim peanut butter, which made a big hit, but even this was invented fourteen years earlier by a St. Louis physician, circa 1890. Yet there were a few firsts nonetheless: Fairy Floss (cotton candy) and puffed rice, which was actually shot from cannons throughout the day, courtesy of the Quarter Oaks exhibit.

These and other tasty wonders delighted visitors who strolled the fair's iconic midway, The Pike, the mile-long main drag of amusements, eateries, restaurants and concessions. Concessionaires hawked culinary handheld classics such as the ice cream cone, which proved to be, as the expression goes, the best thing to come down The Pike. These foods made walking about while eating handheld food socially acceptable, changing the belief that only the ill-bred ate with their fingers.

Quick-food concessionaires weren't the only ones contributing to changing the table at Missouri's only World's Fair. Restaurants, agricultural displays, international exhibits and food companies were bringing new tastes and world flavors to fairgoers—exotic dishes like fried rice and rarities like black olives, kumquats and the new Floridan wonder, the pommelo (later renamed the grapefruit). And let us not forget the staggering number of lunchrooms, eateries and restaurants. A fair favorite was August Lüchow and Tony Faust's Tirolean Alps restaurant, located along The Pike. Its menu had a definitive German accent, offering plates of wiener schnitzel, wurst and sauerkraut—

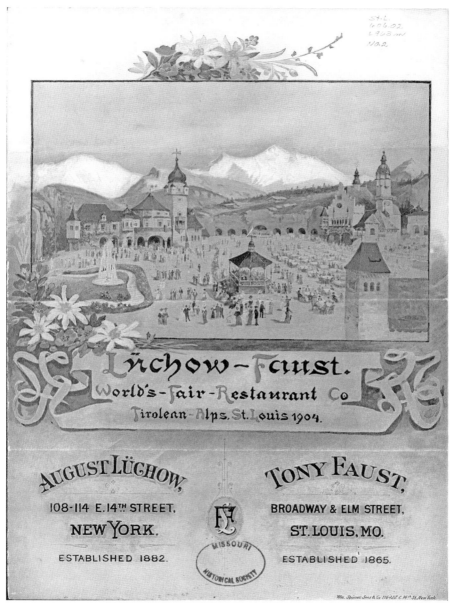

One of the most popular restaurants at the World's Fair was Lüchow-Faust World's Fair Restaurant, located along the Pike within the "Tirolean Alps." *Missouri Historical Society, St. Louis.*

The Hill neighborhood—filled with Italian eateries, bakeries and groceries—is easy to find. Just look for the fire hydrants painted like the Italian flag. *Suzanne Corbett.*

favorites of St. Louis's German community, the largest ethnic group in the city at the time.

When the World's Fair closed, its teardown helped establish one of Missouri's most unique culinary strongholds, the Hill. Dubbed "America's Last Little Italy," it was built near the highest point in St. Louis City, thus explaining the name.

Italians first settled into the neighborhood during the late nineteenth century, working the clay mines. By the turn of the century, more Italians had arrived, and they needed materials to build their houses. The salvage from the fairgrounds offered a solution. Hill residents salvaged the wood, which in turn helped build the neighborhood's shotgun houses.

The Hill became a self-sustaining neighborhood, famous for its Italian food producers like Volpi's (Italian cured meats and sausages), its grocery/importers like J. Viviano & Sons and the numerous family-owned restaurants and restaurateurs like Gian-Tony's and Rich LoRusso. These were just a few of the businesses and passionate people, all proud Italian Americans, who gave Missouri its own unique cuisine, nationally recognized as St. Louis Italian.

From the nineteenth century to the early twentieth century, a dizzying array of new foods came to Missouri's table. Fanciful gourmet creations surfaced on the tables of wealthy families, railroad dining cars delighted hungry passengers and everyone was wowed in 1904 at the St. Louis World's Fair. At the same time, home cooks were getting well-deserved recognition for their skills and recipes at the state fair. It was a time that created an eclectic table mix that's represented by the following recipes.

RECIPES

Chicken à la King
Recipe from *Dining Car Cookbook Manual*, Missouri Pacific Archives

2 tablespoons butter
½ cup julienne-cut pimento or red bell peppers
2 tablespoons flour
1 cup chicken broth
1 cup cream
1 teaspoon rubbed sage leaves
Salt and pepper to taste
1 cup sliced white mushrooms
3 cups diced cooked chicken breasts
½ cup sour cream
¼ cup dry sherry
4 slices white bread, crust removed and toasted
Chopped chives for garnish

1. Melt butter in a large skillet over medium heat. Add pimento and sauté until tender. Remove with a slotted spoon and set aside.
2. Add flour to butter in skillet, whisking out all lumps. Slowly stir in chicken broth and cream.
3. Stir and cook until mixture thickens to a thin gravy consistency.
4. Stir rubbed sage, salt, pepper, mushrooms and chicken breast and cook until bubbly and thickened.

5. Stir in reserved pimento, sour cream and dry sherry. Cook until hot and bubbly. Remove from heat.
6. Cut toast on the diagonal to make toast points, placing two pieces on a serving plate. Spoon the chicken over top and garnish with chopped chives. Makes 4 servings.

Union Pacific Crabmeat à la Louis
Recipe from Union Pacific Archives

½ head romaine lettuce
12 ounces lump crabmeat
2 tomatoes, quartered
2 cooked eggs, quartered
6 ripe olives
¼ cup chili sauce
Dash of Tabasco
2 tablespoons Worcestershire sauce
½ cup mayonnaise
Salt and fresh ground pepper
Lemon wedges

1. Wash and dry romaine. Tear into bite-size pieces or, if leaves are small, leave them whole. Divide between two plates.
2. Top lettuce with crabmeat, placing in the center. Divide and decoratively place the tomatoes, eggs and olives on the plates with the crabmeat.
3. In a bowl, whisk together the chili sauce, Tabasco, Worcestershire and mayonnaise. Season with salt and pepper.
4. Drizzle dressing over top of plated salads, garnish with lemon wedges and serve. Makes 2 salads.

Fred Harvey Railroad Cole Slaw
Recipe from the *Harvey House Cookbook*

¾ cup oil
I cup cider vinegar
I cup sugar
Salt and pepper to taste
I tablespoon celery seed
3 pounds finely shredded green cabbage
I cup finely chopped onions
I green bell pepper, finely chopped
I cup shredded carrots

1. In a small saucepan, combine oil, vinegar, 2 tablespoons of the sugar, salt, pepper and celery seed. Heat together to the boiling point.
2. In a large mixing bowl, combine the cabbage, onions, bell pepper and carrots and mix with remaining sugar. Pour hot dressing over cabbage mixture and toss. Chill overnight or for at least 4 hours before serving. Makes 10 servings.

Creamed Morels
Courtesy Missouri Department of Conservation

2 tablespoons unsalted butter
2 shallots, finely chopped
2 cups fresh (or I cup dried) morels
2 cups heavy cream
Salt and pepper
2 to 3 tablespoons Marsala

1. Melt butter in a skillet over a medium heat; add shallots and sauté for a few minutes.
2. If using fresh morels, cut each in half lengthwise to clean and rinse under running water. If you have large morels, cut them into smaller pieces, but not too small. If using dried morels, reconstitute them in warm water for 15 minutes and then squeeze out the morels, saving the liquid. Cut them into pieces.

3. Add morels to shallots and sauté for 3 to 5 minutes, until all liquid has evaporated.
4. Add cream and cook for a few minutes, until mixture thickens. Season with salt and pepper to taste.
5. Add Marsala and adjust seasonings to taste. Makes 6 to 8 servings.

Hannibal's Pork Tenderloin Sandwich

Recipe based on version made at the Mark Twain Dinette

1-pound boneless pork loin, cut into fourths
2 cups buttermilk
2 eggs
½ cup flour
Salt and pepper to taste
Oil for frying
3 cups plain panko crumbs
4 hamburger buns
Pickles, lettuce and onions

1. Place pork between two pieces of wax paper and pound, using a mallet or rolling pin, to about ¼-inch thickness.
2. In a bowl, whisk together buttermilk, eggs and flour; season with salt and pepper. Add the pork to buttermilk mixture, cover, refrigerate and allow to marinate overnight.
3. Remove pork from refrigerator. Heat about 2 inches of oil in a large cast iron skillet to a medium heat, 350 degrees F.
4. Place crumbs on a shallow plate. Remove cutlets from marinade, shake off excess marinade and then dredge each cutlet in crumbs.
5. Fry in hot oil, about 5 minutes on each side, until golden brown. Remove from skillet and drain on paper towels.
6. Serve the oversized cutlets on toasted hamburger buns with pickles, onions and lettuce on the side. Makes 4 large sandwiches.

Oyster Stew
Recipe from the Campbell House Collection

2 pints oysters, standard size
3 tablespoons butter
2 tablespoons flour
6 to 7 sprigs marjoram or 1 tablespoon fresh marjoram leaves
4 cups half and half
Salt and white pepper to taste

1. Strain oysters in a colander placed over a bowl to catch the liquor. Pick over oysters to remove any pieces of shell.
2. Place oysters with their liquor in a 2½-quart saucepan. Heat over a medium-high heat until oysters' edges begin to curl.
3. Mix together the butter and flour to make a paste, then stir into oysters.
4. Add in marjoram and slowly stir in half and half. Cook over a medium heat until slightly thickened.
5. Season to taste with salt and pepper. Remove marjoram springs before serving.
6. Serve garnished with fresh marjoram or parsley. Makes 6 servings.

Beef Chasseur
Recipe from *The Gilded Table*

3 to 4 garlic cloves, crushed, divided
1½ teaspoons coarse salt
¼ teaspoon fresh ground pepper
3 pounds beef tenderloin, cut into medallions
6 tablespoons butter, divided

For the Sauce:
2 tablespoons brandy
½ cup tomato peeled and chopped or 1 tablespoon tomato paste
2 cloves garlic, minced
¼ cup chopped shallots
½ pound fresh mushrooms, white button or cremini, thinly sliced

3 tablespoons all-purpose flour
1 ½ cups dry red wine
1 cup beef broth
Dash of Worcestershire
1 tablespoon fresh chopped tarragon
Parsley for garnish

1. Combine half the garlic, salt and pepper. Pat the meat slices dry with paper towels and season with the garlic mixture.
2. Sear steak medallions in a large skillet with 2 tablespoons of the butter until browned and cooked to desired doneness. During sautéing, add more butter as needed to prevent pan from burning and skillet becoming too dry.
3. Arrange the steaks on a serving platter. Cover with foil to keep warm while finishing sauce.

To Make Chasseur Sauce:
1. Deglaze sauté pan used for sautéing beef with brandy, scraping bottom to remove caramelized bits stuck on pan.
2. Add 4 tablespoons butter and melt over medium heat. Add tomatoes, garlic and shallots and sauté until softened.
3. Add mushrooms and cook until browned, about 5 minutes. Stir in the flour and reduce heat to low.
4. Whisk in the wine and beef broth; bring to a boil, stirring constantly. Reduce heat and simmer until sauce thickens. Add Worcestershire, tarragon and season to taste with salt and pepper. Makes 6 to 8 servings.

Charlotte Russe
Recipe from *The Gilded Table*

16 to 20 ladyfingers
4 egg yolks
½ cup sugar
1 cup whole milk
1 envelope unflavored gelatin
2 tablespoons cold water
1 tablespoon orange flower water or 2 teaspoons vanilla

2 cups heavy cream
fresh fruit, berries and/or whipped cream (optional garnishes)

1. Split ladyfingers in half and place rounded side down to cover the bottom and sides of a 9-inch springform pan or charlotte mold.
2. In a 2½-quart double boiler, whisk together egg yolks and sugar. Whisk in milk.
3. Place over a medium heat to keep water in bottom half of the double boiler simmering. Cook until mixture thickens to a custard.
4. Dissolve gelatin in the cold water and whisk into custard. Cool custard, but do not allow it set.
5. Once custard is cooled, whisk in orange flower water.
6. Whip cream until stiff and fold into custard. Pour into springform pan or charlotte mold, smoothing top of custard.
7. Refrigerate until custard firmly sets. To serve, remove from pan and garnish with fresh or candied fruits and/or whipped cream. Makes 6 to 8 servings.

Lemon Curd and Cranberry Scones
Recipes are courtesy of Shakespeare Chateau

Lemon Curd
6 tablespoons unsalted butter, softened to room temperature
1 cup sugar
2 large eggs
2 egg yolks
¾ cup lemon juice
1 teaspoon lemon zest

1. In a large bowl, using an electric mixer, beat together butter and sugar for about 2 minutes, until light and fluffy.
2. Beat in the whole eggs, then add the 2 egg yolks, one at a time. Add lemon juice and place into a 2-quart saucepan; cook over a low heat until mixture is smooth.
3. Increase heat to medium, stirring constantly until curd thickens. Do not boil, which can cause curd to separate.
4. Remove lemon curd from heat; stir in lemon zest. Transfer to a canning jar with a lid. Cool to room temperature, then chill and store in refrigerator.

Lemon curd will hold refrigerated for two weeks. Serve with scones or toasted English muffins or use as a filling for cakes and tarts. Makes 2 cups.

Cranberry Scones
2 cups flour
¼ cup sugar
2 teaspoons baking powder
½ teaspoon salt
½ teaspoon lemon zest
6 tablespoons butter, cut into small pieces
½ cup dried cranberries
¾ cup whipping cream
1 egg

1. Heat oven to 425 degrees F.
2. In a large bowl, whisk together flour, sugar, baking powder, salt and lemon zest. With a pastry blender, cut in butter until butter is pea size or smaller, and then add cranberries.
3. Whisk together cream and egg and gently mix into flour mixture to moisten, without overmixing.
4. Turn dough out on a lightly floured surface and gather into two balls. Pat each out to about ¾-inch thickness.
5. Cut each flattened ball in half, then cut each half into three wedge pieces.
6. Place on a greased parchment-lined baking sheet. Bake for 16 to 18 minutes, until golden brown. Serve warm with lemon curd or butter. Makes 12.

J C Wyatt Baked Chocolate Truffle
Recipe courtesy J C Wyatt House

10 ounces coarsely chopped bittersweet chocolate
6 tablespoons unsalted butter
2 eggs, plus 1 yolk, slightly beaten
½ cup heavy cream
3 tablespoons sugar
1 ½ teaspoons vanilla extract

1. Melt the chocolate and butter in a double boiler or a medium-sized heat-proof bowl over barely simmering water, stirring until smooth. Remove chocolate from stove and let cool for about 10 minutes.
2. Gently whisk the eggs, cream, sugar and vanilla together, then slowly whisk into the cooled chocolate.
3. Pour chocolate mixture through a mesh sieve into a medium-sized pitcher or batter bowl. (Straining the mixture removes any bits of egg and large air bubbles.)
4. Heat the oven to 300 degrees F and lightly grease 12 (2-ounce) ramekins.
5. Fill the ramekins to just under the rims and bake for about 20 to 22 minutes, until starting to set. The center should be just a little jiggly.
6. Let cool for 5 minutes and serve, garnished with a berry, a swirl of melted chocolate or a chocolate kiss. Makes 12 servings.

Note: Baked truffles can be chilled and covered for up to 3 days. To serve, bring them to room temperature and warm them in a 200-degree oven for about 5 minutes. 12 servings.

Missouri Paté
Recipe from *Past & Repast: History & Hospitality*
of the Missouri Governor's Mansion

4 tablespoons unsalted butter
½ pound fresh mushrooms, chopped
1 shallot, minced
2 tablespoons bourbon
1 tablespoon cognac
8 ounces liverwurst
2 (8-ounce) packages cream cheese, softened
1 teaspoon fresh dill
1 tablespoon fresh parsley
2 teaspoons Dijon mustard
Salt and freshly ground pepper to taste
Fresh parsley or fresh dill weed for garnish

1. Melt butter in a skillet over a medium-high heat; add mushrooms and shallots and sauté until soft. Stir in bourbon and cognac, then cool.
2. Place mushroom mixture in a food processor with the remaining ingredients and process until smooth.
3. Place paté into a crock or serving bowl. Cover and chill for 24 hours.
4. Garnish paté with either fresh parsley or dill weed. Serve with toasted party rye or French bread and cornichons. Makes 12 servings.

Blue Ribbon Bread and Butter Pickles
Heritage recipe from the Traxel Culinary Collection

8 large cucumbers, thinly sliced
8 small onions, thinly sliced
1 clove garlic
½ cup canning salt
8 cups water
4 cups ice cubes
6 (1-pint) canning jars, with two-piece lids
7 cups sugar
3 cups white vinegar
2 tablespoons mustard seed
1 tablespoon celery seed
2 teaspoons turmeric

1. Place cucumbers and onions in a large bowl or canning kettle. Drop in garlic, sprinkle salt over top and pour water over top.
2. Place ice over top of the cucumbers and allow to stand for 4 hours.
3. Wash canning jars and lids and place in a large kettle. Place on stovetop and cover with water. Heat to a boil, reduce heat and simmer until ready to use.
4. Discard garlic and drain.
5. Place cucumbers and onions in a large canning kettle with sugar, vinegar and spices. Bring ingredients to a boil.
6. Reduce heat and pack pickles into the hot sterilized jars. Leaving a ½ inch of head space, make sure cucumbers are covered with cooking syrup. Slide a knife down the inside of each filled jar to release air bubbles.

7. Wipe jar lid and seal with lid. Place jars in a water bath canner, making sure jars are covered with water. Bring to a boil and process for 10 minutes.
8. Remove jars from water bath and cool. Wipe off jars, tighten lids (if needed) and store in a dark, cool place. Makes 6 pints.

Fresh Concord Grape Pie
Heirloom recipe from the Missouri State Fair

Pastry for two-crust pie
5½ cups fresh Concord grapes
1 cup sugar
¼ cup cornstarch
¼ teaspoon salt
1 teaspoon lemon peel
1 tablespoon grated orange peel
2 tablespoons butter
2 tablespoons cream
2 tablespoons sugar

1. Divide pastry in half and chill. Roll out half of the pastry to fit a 9-inch pie pan. Chill pastry-lined pie pan until ready to fill.
2. Wash grapes and remove skins from each grape by pressing between thumb and forefinger until skin breaks and pulp pops out. Reserve skins.
3. Place grape pulp in a 2-quart saucepan. Heat over medium heat until grape pulp begins to boil. Remove from heat, placing pulp in a wire strainer placed over a bowl. Press pulp through strainer to remove seeds. Discard seeds.
4. Mix the reserved grape skins into the pulp, stir in one cup sugar, cornstarch, salt and peels.
5. Fill the chilled pastry-lined pie pan with the grape mixture and dot top with butter.
6. Heat oven to 425 degrees F. Roll out remaining pastry and cut into 1-by-10-inch strips. Weave pastry strips on top of the pie to make a lattice top.
7. Brush pastry lightly with cream and sprinkle with the remaining sugar.
8. Bake for 40 to 45 minutes or until pastry is golden brown. Makes 1 pie, serving 6 to 8 slices.

Schnitzel à la Holstein
Based on 1904 World's Fair Luchow-Faust Tirolean Alps Restaurant

4 veal cutlets, 4 to 6 ounces each
salt and pepper to taste
6 large eggs
3 tablespoons water
½ cup flour
1 cup finely grated white breadcrumbs
¼ cup butter
¼ cup oil
8 anchovy fillets
1 tablespoons capers
1 lemon

1. Pound veal thin between two pieces of wax paper. Season each side with salt and pepper.
2. In a shallow dish, beat 1 egg with the 3 tablespoons water.
3. Place flour on one plate and the breadcrumbs in another plate.
4. Dredge each piece of veal in flour, shake off the excess, then dip in beaten egg and dip into breadcrumbs to evenly coat each side.
5. Heat butter and oil in a heavy skillet over a medium heat.
6. Place breaded veal slices into the hot oil and brown for a few minutes on each side. Once browned, remove and drain on paper towels and keep warm.
7. In another skillet, fry remaining eggs sunny-side up.
8. To assemble and serve, place a veal cutlet on a plate, top with a fried egg and two anchovies and sprinkle with capers. Serve with lemon wedges. Makes 4 servings.

Homemade Ice Cream Cones
Inspired by vintage nineteenth-century waffle batter recipes

2 egg whites
½ cup sugar

> *3 tablespoons milk*
> *1 teaspoon vanilla*
> *¼ teaspoon salt*
> *⅔ cup flour, sifted*
> *2 tablespoons melted butter*

1. Place egg whites, sugar, milk, vanilla and salt into a mixing bowl and whisk together. Stir in flour and butter, whisking until smooth.
2. Place a nonstick skillet or cast-iron frying pan on medium heat.
3. Pour 2 tablespoons batter into the center of skillet and spread into a 6-inch thin round even layer.
4. Cook for 4 to 5 minutes or until the bottom has browned. Carefully flip over the batter disc and continue to cook for 1 to 2 minutes.
5. Lift the disc off the griddle and quickly roll from the bottom of the cone to shape it. Pull out the shape at the top to make it a wider cone.

Note: The disc will begin to harden almost immediately after leaving the skillet. If a cone proves too hard to shape, make a cone cup by placing disk over an upside-down muffin tin to make a cup shape. Makes 6 to 8 cones.

Nanna's Stuffed Melanzane
Recipe courtesy Rich LoRusso

> *2 eggplants, tops trimmed off, sliced lengthwise into ¼-inch slices*
> *2 tablespoons olive oil, plus more as needed for eggplant*
> *½ cup minced onion*
> *1 tablespoon minced garlic*
> *1 tablespoon fresh basil*
> *1 teaspoon fresh black pepper*
> *½ cup red wine*
> *1 (28-ounce) can whole peeled San Marzano tomatoes, crushed*
> *2 tablespoons tomato paste*
> *¼ cup chopped parsley*
> *2 teaspoons sea salt*
> *1 pound ground chuck*
> *1 pound ground veal*

½ cup minced red onion
½ cup Parmesan cheese
½ cup Italian breadcrumbs
½ teaspoon salt
¼ teaspoon pepper
2 tablespoons whole milk
2 eggs
2 tablespoons minced parsley
½ pound Fontina cheese, cubed
1 yellow sweet bell pepper, deseeded and cut into strips
Parmesan cheese

1. Soak eggplant in salted water for 20 minutes. Drain and place slices on a baking sheet.
2. Lightly brush eggplant slices with olive oil. Bake at 325 degrees F for 10 minutes to soften. Remove from oven and cool.
3. To prepare sauce, heat olive oil in saucepan over medium heat and add onion and garlic; sauté until garlic has lightly browned.
4. Add basil, black pepper, wine, tomatoes, tomato paste, parsley and sea salt; simmer for 20 minutes.
5. To make stuffing, mix ground chuck, ground veal, red onion, Parmesan, breadcrumbs, salt, pepper, whole milk, the eggs and the remaining parsley.
6. Pour half the sauce into a baking dish—a 9x12-inch dish or a casserole.
7. Make an egg-size piece of stuffing and place a cube of the cheese in the center. Place the stuffing/cheese in the center of an eggplant slice, then roll up and place seam side down in the baking dish. Repeat until eggplant slices are stuffed.
8. Pour remaining sauce over top of the rolled eggplant and top each with a strip of yellow pepper.
9. Cover baking dish with foil. Bake at 325 degrees F for 45 minutes, then uncover and continue to bake for 10 minutes.
10. Remove from oven and allow dish to rest for 15 minutes. Top with Parmesan cheese and serve. Makes 6 servings.

Chapter 4

JAZZ, PROHIBITION AND ROUTE 66

P atrons of Lonnie's Reno Club, Kansas City's swanky and swinging jazz spot, are greeted with a Champagne cocktail. It's a taste of the memorable evening ahead of them. Lonnie McFadden—Kansas City's premier jazz entertainer—can do it all: play trumpet, sing, tap dance and tell stories. McFadden, who was raised in Kansas City, is always in command of the room, and this new downtown venue, which opened in November 2020, is the perfect spot for him.

Located on Grand Boulevard, Lonnie's Reno Club is an homage to the original Reno Club from the 1930s that was located at Twelfth and Cherry Streets where jazz greats like Count Basie and his band performed. "History, class, and Kansas City jazz. That's what we do," McFadden said in a recent radio interview.

During the Jazz Age and into the 1930s, Kansas City was the "Paris of the Plains," but across the state in St. Louis, Prohibition hit the city's many breweries hard; unemployment soared during the Great Depression, topping national averages.

In the central part of Missouri, the massive Bagnell Dam project not only created jobs during the start of the 1930s, but it also ushered in a new era for this part of the Ozarks, forever changing how people lived. In Springfield, plans were underway for the Mother Road, a route that would connect a large section of the country and open the new industry of tourism.

NORTHEAST MISSOURI

In the early part of the twentieth century, St. Louis was riding a wave of success. Basking in the glow of the 1904 World's Fair and Olympic Games, the city was expanding its park system and cultural institutions, including its zoo and the outdoor theater known as the Muny, both in Forest Park. By 1918, the city's population was 687,000, earning it the ranking of the fourth-largest municipality in the country, according to *Missouri Medicine*.

During the early 1900s, candy makers, often Greek immigrants, found a home in St. Louis. Connie Mourtoupalas, in a 2020 article for the English edition of *Ekathimerini* (a daily newspaper published in Athens, Greece), wrote, "To say there were thousands of Greek-owned candy shops and ice cream parlors across America is an understatement. By the early 1900s, there were Greek-owned candy and ice cream shops everywhere in the U.S."

In 1913, Harry Karandzieff and his best friend, Pete Jugaloff, emigrated from Greece to St. Louis and opened their candy store/soda fountain at Fourteenth Street and St. Louis Avenue. Harry's grandsons, Andy and Tommy, along with their families, keep Crown Candy Kitchen going at the same north St. Louis neighborhood, making chocolate candies and ice cream treats. The malts are legendary at Crown Candy, the city's oldest soda fountain.

The Mavrakos Candy Company story is also interesting. Greek immigrant John L. Mavrakos settled in St. Louis in 1904 and soon opened a candy and ice cream shop at Vandeventer Avenue and Olive Street. In 1913, Mavrakos and his wife, Madeline, started the Mavrakos Candy Company. The business peaked in the 1950s, when the family had sixteen retail stores in St. Louis and a thriving catalogue business.

But the Mavrakos story ended in 1984 when the company sold to Archibald Candy, based in Chicago. Archibald closed its doors in 2004. Luckily, the Mavrakos family's recipe book was given to Dan Abel, founder of St. Louis's Chocolate Chocolate Chocolate Company, who grew up down the street from Mavrakos's last owner, Tom Wotka. Abel studied the recipes and reinvented a few for his company's product line.

For one hundred years, Merb's Candies has been a part of St. Louis families' celebrations. Opened on South Grand Avenue by Emma Merb in 1921, the business has changed ownership three times. Current owner Teri Bearden said in an interview with the local PBS station that her dad bought the candy shop in the late 1960s after seeing an ad in the *New York Times*. The autumn Bionic Apples that feature her dad's caramel recipe have gained national attention, but it's the heavenly hash with homemade

The Karandzieff family have operated Crown Candy Kitchen in north St. Louis for more than one hundred years. *St. Louis Convention & Visitors Association.*

marshmallow, snappers (turtles) and solid chocolate holiday molds that locals have appreciated for generations.

Eighty-five miles northwest of St. Louis in the small town of Bowling Green, Missouri, Thomas Jefferson Bankhead, the great-grandson of President Thomas Jefferson, started a chocolate shop in 1919 as a spinoff to his successful restaurant in Bowling Green. Over the years, Bankhead's

Candies was passed to several owners, but the candies are still made in large copper kettles, cooled on marble tabletops and dipped by hand.

Then came the ratification of the Eighteenth Amendment in 1919, calling for a nationwide ban on all alcoholic beverages. For a city with an unofficial slogan of "first in shoes, booze, and last in the American League," St. Louis was crushed by Prohibition.

In 1920, there were about three dozen breweries in town, and several—including the once great Lemp Brewery—were forced out of business. Others found ways to remain opening by manufacturing other products. Anheuser-Busch produced yeast and a near beer called "Bevo," while Falstaff Corporation (formerly Griesedieck Beverage) produced a near beer and IBC Root Beer. Today, Anheuser-Busch is under the global AB InBev umbrella and Falstaff went out of production, but IBC Root Beer is still made, but by a different company.

Missouri breweries weren't the only companies affected by Prohibition. In his book *Exploring Missouri Wine Country*, author Brett Dufur noted that Missouri had more than one hundred wineries prior to Prohibition. Stone Hill Winery in Hermann, Missouri, was the second largest in the country. Wine production was closed, but owners used the network of underground cellars to grow mushrooms. However, St. Stanislaus Seminary's vineyards survived because Jesuits produced sacramental wine on site. The seminary in north St. Louis County closed in 1971.

Other companies saw opportunities to jump on the beverage bandwagon. Vess Beverage Company, founded in 1916 in St. Louis by Sylvester Jones, had a variety of flavored soft drinks. Its popular Whistle orange soda was formulated by employee Charles Leiper Grigg, but he and Jones had a falling out; Grigg left Vess—and Whistle orange soda—to work briefly for the Warner-Jenkinson Company, where he developed an orange-flavored soft drink called Howdy. In 1920, Grigg left that company, this time with his soda formula, and formed the Howdy Company with Edmund G. Ridgway (financier) and Frank Gladney (attorney) in 1921.

Grigg worked on a new formula for a lemon-lime drink that contained a mood-altering component, lithium citrate. The beverage, launched just weeks before the stock market crash in 1929, was called Bib-Label Lithiated Lemon-Lime Soda. The name was changed to 7 Up Lithiated Lemon Soda and, thankfully, shortened to simply 7UP in 1936. The lithium citrate was removed from the formula in 1948.

In spite of the Eighteenth Amendment, Americans were finding ways to wet their whistles. Bootleg booze and speakeasies had a stronghold in St.

Louis. By 1931, St. Louis had three thousand "beer flats" in addition to more than one thousand speakeasies, according to an article in the S*t. Louis Globe-Democrat.* James Dillon, assistant deputy Prohibition administrator, also suspected that restaurants and confectioneries regularly dispensed liquor.

Illegally made booze also came into St. Louis from other parts of the state. Authorities seized six thousand gallons of beer from the Appleton Brewery in Cape Girardeau County in southeast Missouri. According to the story in the *St. Louis Post-Dispatch* (May 27, 1932), the brewery—no stranger to federal raids—supplied St. Louis speakeasies. The beer was being sold in St. Louis for twenty-five dollars per half barrel, and the speakeasies would resell to patrons for twenty-five cents per stein (about sixty dollars per half barrel).

Like bootleg beer, jazz flowed freely in St. Louis. With the music rooted in ragtime around the turn of the century, venues along Market Street welcomed talented musicians like blues/jazz trumpeter Charles Creath. Many musicians played popular music on the Strekfus excursion boats that traveled up and down the Mississippi River. The boats ran afternoon sightseeing cruises, but in the evening, patrons danced to live orchestras.

By 1931, it seemed as though the only folks with jobs were bootleggers. In these early years of the Great Depression, St. Louis's unemployment rate was steadily climbing and would reach 30 percent, well above the national average, by 1933. Several thousand displaced people made an encampment called Hooverville (in a nod to President Herbert Hoover) along the banks of the Mississippi River. The charitable Welcome Inn provided Hooverville residents with meager meals plus day-old bread and rejected vegetables.

In 1931, a widowed St. Louis housewife trying to earn money to avoid financial ruin published a cookbook that would become a staple in American kitchens. Irma Starkloff Rombauer's *The Joy of Cooking* has sold more than 18 million copies since its debut. In 1936, its groundbreaking "action method" recipe format could teach even the clumsiest of cooks how to find joy in the kitchen.

That same year, Louis Kaufman opened his potato chip company Old Vienna Snack Food Company in St. Louis. The company's spicy Red Hot Riplets are ridge-cut potato chips generously covered in a chili pepper/barbecue–style seasoning. The company changed ownership several times over the years, but it was dissolved in 1996 and brought back as Old Vienna LLC.

It was also during the 1930s that one of St. Louis's culinary gifts to the country was created—though quite by accident. It's believed that a German baker, in an attempt to create a yellow cake, screwed up the topping, adding too much butter and sugar. Not wanting to waste any ingredients, the cake wasn't tossed, and what some would see as a sticky mess would become Gooey Butter Cake, an item still made and sold today in St. Louis.

Northwest Missouri

By 1920, jazz cabarets were jumping and whiskey was freely flowing in Kansas City. Once regarded as a western cow town, Kansas City was emerging as the "Paris of the Plains," a moniker derived from an article by George Miller, editor of the *Omaha Herald*, who wrote, "If you want to see some sin, forget about Paris. Go to Kansas City."

Breweries and distilleries have existed in the city since the nineteenth century. Muehlebach Brewing Company began operating in 1869 and produced 100,000 barrels of beer in 1911, earning it the title as the second-largest brewer in the city, just behind Kansas City Breweries Company.

Holladay Distillery in nearby Weston, Missouri, had been in operation since 1856, while Kansas City's J. Rieger & Company, prior to being shuttered in 1920 by the Eighteenth Amendment and federal Prohibition, was the largest producer of mail-order whiskey in the country.

Although there were some casualties among the city's brewers and distilleries, Thomas J. "Boss Tom" Pendergast made sure that the booze and good times kept flowing in his city. In 1920, Pendergast bought the Pabst Building, using it to bottle and distribute Pabst beer. However, he sold near beer and bottled water from that location as well, and it was widely believed that this was the spot from which Boss Tom ran this bootleg liquor operation. (Today, the building in the trendy Crossroads District is the boutique Crossroads Hotel.)

Bootlegging wasn't the only business for the powerful Pendergast political machine, which was started by James F. Pendergast, Tom's elder brother. The Pendergast Years, a project between the Kansas City Public Library and the Center for Midwestern Studies (University of Missouri–Kansas City), lists more than a dozen companies owned or financed by Pendergast. The diverse collection involved liquor, coal, financial, asphalt and concrete businesses.

The 1920s and 1930s were a defining era for Kansas City. In his book *Prohibition in Kansas City, Missouri: Highballs, Spooners & Crooked Dice*, author John Simonson noted that this was a period of rapid growth in population, industry, culture and construction. According to Simonson, by 1929, there were sixty buildings over ten stories tall. This nineteenth-largest city had America's eighth-tallest skyline.

This buzzing atmosphere in Kansas City attracted creative people, including Ernest Hemingway, who worked as a young reporter at the *Kansas City Star* from October 1917 to April 1918. In 1922, Walt Disney opened his first animation studio, Laugh-O-Gram Films, on East Thirty-First Street, although the business failed about a year later. Of course, Disney's story has a very happy ending.

This also was the era of the Kansas City Monarchs, one of the charter teams of baseball's Negro Leagues. The Monarchs took ten league championships and won the first Negro League World Series in 1924. From the harsh reality of segregation, the Monarchs launched the careers of baseball legends, including Jackie Robinson, who was recruited in 1945 by the Brooklyn Dodgers. Other legends included Ernie Banks, Cool Papa Bell, Satchel Paige and Kansas City's greatest baseball ambassador, Buck O'Neil. The Negro League Baseball Museum remembers this era.

Jazz provided the soundtrack for what was happening in Kansas City. With roots in ragtime and blues, there was a distinct Kansas City sound that was being developed by pioneering musicians such as Bennie Moten, who made one of the city's first jazz recordings in 1923. Sections of the city—including Twelfth Street and Eighteenth and Vine—boasted large concentrations of cabarets, dance halls and speakeasies. At one time, fifty clubs lined Twelfth Street alone—including the original Reno Club—and more than one hundred venues hosted jazz greats like Count Basie, Joe Turner and local legend Charlie Parker, who was born in 1920 in Kansas City, Kansas, and raised on the Missouri side.

Along with its jazz and boss politics, Kansas City's barbecue culture was also jumping at this time, although the practice of slowly smoked meats had been a part of the city since the nineteenth century. When the Hannibal Bridge opened in 1869, the *Daily Journal of Commerce* reported that the occasion was met with a parade and a barbecue. Similarly, when a section of Fort Scott Railroad was completed in 1880, a "grand barbecue" was held in the southern part of the city, according to a story in the *Kansas City Star* (then the *Evening Star*).

Henry Perry is recognized as Kansas City's king of barbecue. Perry, formerly of Memphis, Tennessee, came to Kansas City in 1907 and started a barbecue stand soon after relocating. By 1910, he had enough funds to open an "eat shop," considered Kansas City's first barbecue restaurant. A Black-owned business was listed in the city directory from 1908 to 1924: "Henry

Perry, Barbecue King," at 1514 East Nineteenth Street near the Eighteenth and Vine African American neighborhood.

Kansas City's stockyards provided meat that was relatively affordable, and Perry smoked pork and beef on his outdoor pit—as well as an occasional opossum or raccoon. The variety of meats along with dry rubs and a tomato/molasses-based sauce are hallmarks of Kansas City barbecue. By the early 1930s, Eighteenth and Vine had more than one hundred barbecue restaurants.

At the time of his death in 1940, Perry had three successful barbecue restaurants, according to an article in *Feast* magazine. Charlie Bryant managed one of the enterprises, and when Perry died, the restaurant was left to Bryant, and when he died, his younger brother, Arthur, took over the reins. The original location on Brooklyn Avenue still serves Arthur's signature barbecued ribs with his secret sauce.

George and Arzelia Gates bought a neglected barbecue joint, Ol' Kentucky Bar-B-Q, in 1946. Arthur Pinkard, a cook and former student of Perry's, "came with the place," according to Carolyn Wells, cofounder of the Kansas City Barbeque Society. "He [Pinkard] taught the Gates family how to barbecue the Henry Perry way. Arthur retired and left town in the early 1950s," Wells said. Although Kansas City is one of four official categories of American barbecue (along with Carolina, Memphis and Texas), Wells said that Kansas City is "the melting pot of barbecue."

No matter where you stop for barbecue in Kansas City, you have to get a side of burnt ends, which originated here. These tender, smoky, caramelized pieces of beef brisket are usually served on white bread. And when you bite into that tasty sandwich, remember Otto Rohwedder, inventor of the first bread-slicing machine, and the Chillicothe Baking Company.

Rohwedder, born in Iowa, relocated to St. Joseph, Missouri, after marrying his wife, Catherine. Although he owned three jewelry stores in town, Rohwedder believed that he could invent a machine to slice and wrap bread. He sold his businesses to fund his idea, and in 1927, the design was finished. He sold the first machine to his friend and baker Frank Bench, and in 1928, the Chillocothe Baking Company sold the first loaf of machine-sliced bread in Chillothe, Missouri.

St. Joseph, Missouri, in the 1920s also had a piece of the Jazz Age story, while helping to feed America's sweet tooth. Saxophonist Coleman Hawkins was born in 1904 in St. Joseph. While a high school student, Hawkins was invited to stand in with the Jazz Hounds in Kansas City, the band for blues/jazz singer Mamie Smith. He went on tour with the band in 1922 before

Barbecue lovers enjoy ribs, burnt ends and other perfectly smoked meats at Arthur Bryant's Barbeque. *Jason Dailey/Visit KC.*

leaving about a year later for New York City. Hawkins went on to become a bebop pioneer and had a successful recording and touring career with his own orchestra.

While Hawkins was touring with the Jazz Hounds, Chase Candy Company opened a large headquarters building in his hometown. Makers of the popular Cherry Mash candy bar, Chase by 1926 was manufacturing more than five hundred varieties of candy and had more than four hundred employees. But the Great Depression hit Chase Candy hard, and sales plummeted. The company was bought in the early 1940s by F.S. Yantis & Company, which continues to manufacture the Cherry Mash bar, as well as peanut candies.

CENTRAL MISSOURI

Say "central Missouri" to any resident of the Show-Me State and you'll likely receive a variety of responses. Those who love fishing and water recreation will probably name the Lake of the Ozarks. History buffs or those who follow politics might name Jefferson City, the state capital. College graduates will recall their years at Columbia College, Stephens College or the University of Missouri–Columbia (also known as Mizzou) in Columbia, Missouri's fourth-largest city.

By the turn of the twentieth century, a vibrant downtown was forming in Columbia to support residents and visitors. The Missouri Kansas & Texas Railroad completed the Columbia spur in 1899. Columbia's three hotels were ready to welcome its passengers.

In 1901, a new newspaper, the *Columbia Daily Tribune*, listed thirty-five businesses in town. The majority were grocers, but saloons, billiard halls, bakeries and restaurants also were included. One of those businesses, Booches—a restaurant and billiard hall—is still in operation. It's known for good hamburgers.

Area lumber and brick businesses supported building construction, including city hall. The automobile brought more people through Columbia and another business district developed off Highway 40 (now Interstate 70), but that didn't weaken Columbia's downtown; it remains a busy district for retail, entertainment and dining.

One of the city's oldest restaurants, Ernie's Café and Steakhouse, has served up comforting classics since 1934. Stop in the Art Deco building on East Walnut for its "Chopped Cow," which is a double burger. This sandwich was a favorite of Chester Gould, the *Dick Tracy* comic strip creator. His daughter attended Stephens College in the 1940s, and when Gould came to town for a visit, he often ate at Ernie's. Locals swear that this is the best place for breakfast in town.

Another downtown business, Central Dairy, got its start in Columbia in 1920. Dot Sappington and Clyde Shephard operated in Columbia until 1932, when Sappington sold his shares to start a new Central Dairy in Jefferson City. That location's iconic ice cream parlor was added in the 1940s. While both locations shared the same logo and name, they operated separately. In 1959, the Columbia location was sold. Central Dairy's ice cream parlor under the familiar red-and-white awning remains a popular spot that generations of Missourians have enjoyed. Few people can resist popping into Central Dairy while visiting Jefferson City for business or during a day trip for a cone, sundae, malt or ice cream soda. In April and May, busloads of elementary school kids often finish the annual field trip to the state capitol with a stop for ice cream.

Jefferson City was created to be Missouri's capital. Incorporated in 1825, the state assembly relocated from St. Charles, Missouri, to the new location in 1826. But fire destroyed that capitol in 1837 and a second was completed in 1840, although it, too, was lost to a fire in 1911. The current structure was completed in 1917. Other public buildings in Jefferson City, such as the state Supreme Court building, date to the early 1900s.

During Prohibition, folks could easily find liquor in Jefferson City and Cole County. According to the *Jefferson City News-Tribune*, bootleggers knew the right people to pay off and, for the most part, were left alone to sell their booze. Raids were sometimes conducted for political purposes, but central Missourians knew that Jefferson City was open for business.

Capitol Brewery Company, however, was affected by Prohibition. The successful brewery, which was founded in 1892, had to come up with a new business plan once the Eighteenth Amendment went into effect. Brothers Jacob W. and Ernst Moerschel (sons of founder Jacob F. Moerschel) bottled various soft drinks, delivered ice and coal and even offered their cold storage to grocers under the new company name of Moerschel Products Company. In 1922, the brothers invested in a franchise license to bottle Coca-Cola.

When Prohibition was lifted, the brewery went back into the beer business, but due to stiff competition, it stopped production in 1947. The company—now called the Jefferson City Coca-Cola Bottling Company—continued bottling the soft drink until 2001. Distribution services today are housed in the historical building.

The central Missouri Ozarks was an area untouched by big business and politics until the late 1920s and 1930s. "Before 1931, people lived on farms in a mostly cashless society," said Ken Van Landuyt, coauthor of the book *A People's History of the Lake of the Ozarks*. In the work, Van Landuyt and Dan William Peek share how people living in the Ozark hills grew or caught what they ate, traveled on foot or maybe by horse-drawn wagons and were educated in country schools. Hogs roamed freely and were frequently hunted for meat. River fish were caught by hand in a practice known locally as noodling.

When railroads came to towns such as Versailles and Bagnell, a demand for cut timber to make rail ties put some people to work, but the majority still lived off the land. Everything changed when Walter P. Cravens formed the Missouri Hydro-Electric Power Company in the mid-1920s to dam the Osage River to provide electricity to Kansas City and St. Louis.

Van Landuyt and Peek go into great (and fascinating) detail about how this was accomplished while providing employment opportunities to build Bagnell Dam and support the small city of workers that had cropped up. "There was not a [Great] Depression in this area. Up to 4,000 people would be employed on any given day," Van Landuyt said in a KCUR radio interview in 2018.

Construction of the dam started in 1929 and was finished two years later. When the dam opened for traffic on May 30, 1931, tourists jammed hotels, prompting residents to open their homes up to visitors, according to a historian's account that's part of the book. The impoundment was christened Lake of the Ozarks and was the largest man-made lake in the country at the time. With more than 1,100 miles of shoreline and fifty-four thousand surface acres, the lake attracts more than 5 million visitors per year, according to the Lake of the Ozarks Convention & Visitors Bureau.

Southeast Missouri

One tourist stop in Cape Girardeau is an 1,100-foot-long mural along the city's flood wall. Twenty-four colorful panels visually depict some historic moments in Missouri and southeast Missouri history. Tragic tales—such as the Trail of Tears, the Civil War, the fire in 1916 that destroyed most of downtown and the big flood of 1927—are told alongside moments of jubilation, including President William Howard Taft's visit in 1909.

With about forty thousand residents, "the Cape" is the biggest city in the region and is home to Southeast Missouri State University. By contrast, the poorest county (Shannon) in the state is about two and a half hours west. There's a lot of history to discover in southeast Missouri, but you have to dig for it. In terms of food traditions, this region decidedly borrows from the South. In fact, the southernmost part of the state, Missouri's Bootheel, almost became a part of Arkansas. Small cities—such as Sikeston, Kennett and Poplar Bluff—are scattered through an area that's remained largely very rural.

"Missouri's Bootheel was still very much the Laura Ingalls Wilder–esque frontier until the mid-twentieth century," said Adam Criblez, associate professor in the Department of History and Anthropology at Southeast Missouri State University. Criblez also is director of the Bollinger Center for Regional History on the university's campus. A memoir published by the center depicts a way of life that relied on neighbors and living off the land.

In *The Way It Was in Southeast Missouri*, Luella Duncan tells of growing up in Puxico, Missouri. Duncan, who was born in 1916 on her grandparents' farm, recalled stories that her grandmother shared of family members who fought in the Civil War. Her grandma never knew cousins "who were Yankees." Tea was made by boiling sassafras roots, wild greens were collected and cooked for lunch, neighborhood hog killings were held and gardens produced a variety of berries and vegetables. When it was time to harvest wheat at a nearby farm, the whole community celebrated and helped. "Everybody in the community looked forward to Liley's wheat threshing," Duncan wrote. "The men would come with their teams of horses…the women would come to help Mrs. Liley cook…and there would be fifty or sixty people for the noon meal."

Cotton, which had been grown in Missouri since before the Civil War, was another cash crop for this region. The sharecropping system was far from equitable, often leading to racial violence in the early decades of the twentieth century. In 1939, sharecroppers—Black and White—walked off the farms in protest because landowners were not sharing New Deal subsidies to cut back on farm production with their workers. Lining visible highways, the striking workers were deemed to be "public health hazards" by Governor Lloyd Stark, who ordered the demonstrators moved to isolated areas. The demonstration faded, but not before they caught greater attention in Missouri and Washington, D.C., causing Eleanor Roosevelt to pick up the fight, which helped to facilitate a meeting between President Franklin D. Roosevelt and the strike's organizer, Reverend Owen Whitfield. Eventually, Stark and Whitfield met as well, and social service programs for sharecroppers would be the result of this momentum. Cotton today continues to be one of southeast Missouri's crops, alongside rice, soybeans and corn.

Drive through or tour southeast Missouri and there's a good chance you'll stop at Lambert's Café in Sikeston. Earl and Agnes Lambert borrowed money to start their business in 1942; it takes a good amount of gumption to launch a restaurant during wartime food rationing. But their eight-table restaurant opened, and over the years, diners have learned to love the southern-style victuals and the famous "throwed rolls." Now, after two expansions in Sikeston—plus locations near Branson, Missouri, and Foley, Alabama—Lambert's has become a road trip legend. Here's a bit of trivia: the ovens crank out about 520 dozen hot rolls per day, from 9:00 a.m. to 9:00 p.m.

During World War II, Camp Weingarten—one of four prisoner of war camps—was located in southeast Missouri outside Ste. Geneviève. Some entered the local workforce due to labor shortages. Prisoners of war who were dispatched to smaller camps, such as the one in Sikeston, did basic farm work. In his book *The Enemy Among Us: POWs in Missouri During World War II*, author David Fiedler retells a story of an Italian prisoner who, upon returning to Italy, wrote to the Sikeston farmer for whom he worked, stating that he had enjoyed the job. The farmer didn't respond, but his daughter did, which eventually resulted in a marriage.

SOUTHWEST MISSOURI

Moonshine, tomatoes and the beginnings of Route 66 are part of southwest Missouri's early twentieth-century story. Many men living in Missouri's southern Ozarks, with its Scotch-Irish heritage, possessed distilling skills. This, coupled with plentiful corn and plenty of hiding places in the hills, created opportunities for moonshiners. The demand for moonshine naturally peaked during the years of Prohibition. But another commodity, tomatoes, had a bigger impact on the region.

The southern Ozarks of Missouri had clusters of small farms. These farmers produced a variety of crops and were able to eke out a modest living for their families. Tomato canning fit well into this lifestyle. As Americans became more comfortable with canned foods in the later years of the nineteenth century, canneries became more common. From this time up until the early years following World War II, millions of cases of canned tomatoes were picked and processed in the Ozarks. By 1900, Ozark canneries were supplying 20 percent of tomatoes for the country, exporting to as many as sixteen surrounding states. Brokers in 1910 sold Ozark tomatoes for a 2 percent commission.

The majority of these tomatoes were picked and processed on small farms, as struggling families saw this as a solid sideline business, but there were several commercial canneries in the area, including Ozark Mountain and Red Gold tomatoes in Springfield. Workers in the canneries were paid an average of six dollars per week in the early 1900s, working from July to October. The canning facilities were usually crowded and hot, but there was money in "red gold," and the work continued.

According to an article by Tom Dicke written for the Agricultural History Society, by 1908 there were one hundred tomato canneries in Webster County just east of Springfield, most of which were on small farms. But as these small Ozark farms disappeared, so did the tomato canning industry. One of the last canneries operated into the 1960s at the College of the Ozarks near Branson because of its availability of student labor through its work-study program.

During Prohibition, bootlegging liquor became a profitable business in southwest Missouri. Spring-fed streams were plentiful in the Ozark Mountains, and it was not uncommon to find a moonshiner's still near the source; however, water sometimes had to be piped in from a nearby stream. Most of the time, moonshine was made for personal consumption, but with Prohibition, the demand exploded in the 1920s and 1930s. An article in the *Joplin Globe* noted that whiskey made in the Ozarks could bring in twelve dollars per gallon. Corn at this time was worth more by the gallon than by the bushel.

In an *Ozarks Watch* magazine article, Curtis Copeland wrote that the town of Chadwick in the eastern part of Christian County was the center of the moonshine industry. Neighbors often protected the moonshine makers from law enforcement, and stores openly sold supplies needed to make bootleg liquor, which was shipped as far north as Chicago, Illinois.

Even after Prohibition, Ozark moonshiners kept their whiskey flowing. For the most part, moonshiners and the local law were on friendly terms. However, moonshining was taken much more seriously by federal agents, and raiding stills could be dangerous work. The Joplin newspaper noted that between 1920 and 1983, 196 agents were killed in the line of duty.

The 1920s also saw the birth of the now legendary Route 66. Missouri voters approved a bond issue for much-needed road improvements. In 1926, a telegram from a Springfield hotel was sent to federal officials stating that the numerical designation of 66 was preferred over the proposed 62 for the road that would stretch from Chicago to Los Angeles. As a result, Springfield is recognized as the birthplace of Route 66. The following year, the US Highway 66 Association was founded, with John T. Woodruff, a Springfield attorney, as its first president. By 1931, the Missouri portion of the route from St. Louis to Joplin had been completely paved.

During the 1940s, more businesses such as motels, gas stations and restaurants dotted the highway to accommodate folks heading west. Petroleum engineer Walter Ott and his wife, Ruby, opened a restaurant along Route 66 in the 1940s in Carthage. *The Route 66 St. Louis Cookbook* by Norma Maret Bolin tells the story of how Walter used his background in chemistry to re-create his mom's salad dressing for the restaurant. The French-style salad dressing with horseradish became so popular that the Ott family closed the restaurant in 1948 to commercially make and distribute the dressing. The company still is located in Carthage and makes a variety of sauces and dressings.

Although Route 66 represented opportunity and freedom for some, African Americans knew that traveling from Chicago through Missouri and beyond could be potentially dangerous. To help Black travelers, Black postal worker Victor Green published a guide, *The Negro Motorist Green Book*, starting in 1936 and continuing into the 1960s.

In her book *Overground Railroad: The Green Book and the Roots of Black Travel in America*, author Candacy Taylor recounts through exhaustive research (including scouting more than four thousand sites) and personal narratives what it was like for African Americans to travel across America. Working with the National Park Service, Taylor also compiled a list of *Green Book* businesses along the route. Springfield once had a hotel, inns, guest houses and other businesses that welcomed Black visitors. Carthage and Joplin had a handful of private homes that took in travelers for the night. Most of these sites have been demolished.

Many other businesses along Missouri's route have also been lost to time, but a handful remain. In Lebanon, for example, the Munger Moss Hotel, which opened in 1946, has been restored to its vintage charm. Wrinks Market, which was in business from 1950 to 2005, remains in the family. On most days, Katie Hapner, granddaughter of the original owner, Glenn Winkle, is at the store. The Manor House Inn, built in 1903, was a private home that was turned into a motel in 1932 and operated until 1975. Owners in 2018 restored the home to its former glory to welcome guests again. Lebanon also is home to the Route 66 Museum and Research Center.

Springfield had one of the first drive-in restaurants along Route 66, Red's Giant Hamburg. Known for its hamburgers, the "er" was lopped off the original sign due to power lines. The current Red's restaurant opened in 2019 with the similar vintage look. Rail Haven Motel, which dates to 1938,

Best Western Rail Haven motel is a real slice of Route 66 in Springfield, Missouri. *Springfield CVB.*

has been restored while retaining the vintage Route 66 vibe and is now part of the Best Western chain.

The Parkmoor Drive-In in Webster Groves (a St. Louis suburb) is a reimagined version of the legendary Route 66 restaurant that closed in 1999. Many fondly remember the restaurant's onion rings, which the Parkmoor's co-owner Frank Romano has included on the menu.

The Big Chief Roadhouse in Wildwood, another St. Louis suburb, is one of the last remaining full-service restaurants along Missouri's Route 66.

RECIPES

Spinach-Artichoke Stuffed Portobello Mushrooms
Recipe from Stone Hill Winery. While not stated in original recipe, look for 10-ounce frozen chopped spinach and a 14-ounce can of artichoke hearts.

2 small shallots, diced
2 packages frozen spinach, thawed and drained
1¾ cups mayonnaise
1½ cups feta cheese, crumbled
2 cups breadcrumbs
2 egg whites
1 teaspoon white pepper
1 can artichoke hearts, drained and chopped
Dash cayenne pepper
12 portobello mushrooms

1. Preheat oven to 375 degrees F.
2. Sauté shallots in a small amount of butter. Mix with the rest of the ingredients except the mushrooms.
3. Remove ribs from mushrooms and fill with stuffing mixture. Bake for 7 to 10 minutes. Makes 12 appetizer portions.

7UP® Bundt Cake

Recipe from Dr Pepper/Seven Up Inc. By adding the effervescent soda to the batter, the cake becomes super light in texture; serve with sherbet or fresh fruit.

1 ½ cups butter
3 cups sugar
2 tablespoons lemon extract
5 eggs
3 cups all-purpose flour
¾ cup 7UP
3 ¼ cups powdered sugar
1 teaspoon vanilla
3 tablespoons lemon juice
¼ cup cold 7UP

1. Preheat oven to 325 degrees F.
2. Using an electric hand mixer, beat the sugar and butter together until creamy.
3. Add lemon extract and mix.
4. Add eggs and mix.
5. Add flour and mix.
6. Add 7UP and mix for 1 minute.
7. Scrape down sides of bowl.
8. Mix for 1 minute at low speed.
9. Pour batter into a greased Bundt pan. Bake for 1 hour or until toothpick comes out clean.
10. To make the glaze, use an electric mixer to combine powdered sugar, vanilla, lemon juice and the cold 7UP. Beat until smooth.
11. Let cake stand in the pan to cool for 10 minutes. Turn cake over onto a plate and remove from pan. Let cake cool before drizzling with the glaze. Makes 6 to 8 servings.

St. Louis Gooey Butter Cake

Recipe from the *St. Louis Post-Dispatch* Recipe Exchange column, November 2008. It was noted that the yeast dough base is similar to what professional bakers use.

¼ cup whole milk, heated to 100 degrees F
1½ teaspoons instant or rapid-rise yeast
¼ cup granulated sugar
2 large eggs, room temperature
½ teaspoon vanilla extract
½ teaspoon salt
1½ cups all-purpose flour
6 tablespoons unsalted butter, cut into 6 pieces and softened
½ cup granulated sugar
4 tablespoons unsalted butter, softened
2 ounces cream cheese, softened
2 tablespoons light corn syrup
1 large egg, at room temperature
1 teaspoon vanilla
⅓ cup all-purpose flour
3 tablespoons instant vanilla pudding mix
2 tablespoons powdered sugar

Squares of gooey butter cake have been a St. Louis favorite for generations. *Deborah Reinhardt.*

1. Adjust oven rack to lower-middle position and preheat oven to 200 degrees F. When the oven reaches this temperature, shut it off. Line an 8-inch square baking pan with a sheet of foil that extends over two edges. Grease foil and a medium oven-safe bowl.

2. To prepare the dough, in the bowl of a standing mixer (use paddle attachment if you have one) mix milk and yeast on low speed until yeast dissolves. Add sugar, eggs, vanilla, salt and flour; mix until combined, about 30 seconds. Increase speed to medium-low and add butter, one piece at a time, until incorporated. Continue mixing for 5 minutes.

3. Transfer batter to the greased bowl and place in warm oven. Let rise until doubled in size, about 30 minutes. Spread batter in prepared baking pan. Preheat oven to 350 degrees F.
4. To prepare topping, in a standing mixer (use paddle attachment if you have one), beat granulated sugar, butter and cream cheese on medium speed until light and fluffy (about 2 minutes). Reduce speed to low; add corn syrup, egg and vanilla until combined. Add flour and pudding mix; beat until just incorporated. Portion dollops of topping completely over batter. Spread into an even layer.
5. Bake in preheated oven until exterior is golden and the center of the topping is just beginning to color (center should jiggle slightly when the pan is shaken), about 25 minutes. Cool in pan at least 3 hours. Use foil overhang to lift cake from pan and dust cake with powdered sugar. Yields 9 portions.

St. Louis–Style Street Corn
Recipe from Old Vienna LLC. This dish features fresh summer sweet corn and a zippy dressing that includes Red Hot Riplets Seasoning.

2 slices bacon
1 teaspoon Red Hot Riplets Seasoning
2 tablespoons mayonnaise
1 tablespoon fresh lime juice (approximately 1 lime)
3 cups fresh corn kernels (approximately 4 ears, shucked)
Kosher salt
2 cloves garlic, minced or grated
1 jalapeño, stemmed, seeded and diced
2 green onions, chopped, including green tops
2 ounces Cotija or feta cheese, crumbled
¼ cup fresh cilantro, finely chopped
1 bag of Old Vienna Red Hot Riplets
Extra cheese and cilantro for garnish, if desired

1. In a large skillet, cook bacon until crisp. Reserve 2 tablespoons of bacon grease. Set bacon aside.

2. Combine Old Vienna Red Hot Riplet Seasoning with mayonnaise and lime juice. Set aside.
3. Add corn kernels to skillet with bacon grease. Add salt to taste. Cook over medium-high heat without moving the corn around for two minutes per side, flipping corn four times (total 8 minutes), until charred. Transfer to large serving bowl.
4. Dress with mayonnaise mixture and add garlic, jalapeño, green onions, cheese, cilantro and crumbled bacon. Mix well. Top with a handful of crumbled Red Hot Riplets. Add extra cheese and cilantro for garnish if desired. Yields 4 portions.

Horsefeather
(This cocktail recipe comes from J. Rieger & Co., a distillery based in Kansas City, Missouri. With a history that dates to 1887, the original distillery closed in 1919 due to Prohibition. The brand was brought back in 2014 with the first release of Rieger's Kansas City Whiskey.)

1 ½ ounces Rieger's KC Whiskey
4 ounces Cock'n Bull Ginger Beer
4 or 5 heavy dashes of Angostura aromatic bitters
Lemon wedge

Combine the whiskey and ginger beer in a Collins glass with ice. Float bitters across the top of the cocktail and garnish with a lemon wedge.

Kansas City–Style Brisket Burnt Ends
Recipe courtesy of the Kansas City Barbeque Society (KCBS), an international organization of barbecue and grilling enthusiasts represented by members from every U.S. state and forty-five countries.

1 (4- to 5-pound) beef brisket, point cut
Dry rub of choice
Barbecue sauce of choice

Burnt ends, a classic Kansas City barbecue dish, often are served on bread. *istock.com.*

1. Heat smoker to 250 degrees F.
2. Trim away all the fat cap from brisket and season liberally with dry rub. Smoke brisket for 5 hours.
3. Remove meat, wrap in aluminum foil and return to smoker. Cook until interior reaches 210 degrees on instant-read thermometer, approximately 2 hours.
4. Remove brisket, still wrapped in foil, and allow to stand for 15 minutes.
5. Unwrap brisket, reserving drippings and move meat to cutting board. Slice into 1-inch cubes.
6. Coat the cubed meat with drippings and then glaze with barbecue sauce. Reheat for 15 minutes in smoker in foil or pan. Serve burnt ends with white bread.

Note: KCBS recommends either oak or pecan for smoking brisket. Use two or three chunks. Cooks without a backyard smoker may place charcoal and wood chunks to one side of the kettle, placing the brisket on the other side.

Central Dairy's Best Potato Salad Ever
Recipe from Central Dairy in Jefferson City, Missouri.

5 pounds unpeeled red potatoes
1 large red onion, roughly chopped
1 pound thick-cut bacon, fried and crumbled
1 cup shredded cheddar cheese
2 cups Central Dairy sour cream
1 cup mayonnaise
1 tablespoon garlic powder
1 teaspoon smoked chipotle Tabasco sauce
2 tablespoons steak seasoning
2 teaspoons Worcestershire sauce
Salt and pepper to taste
Chives, diced, for garnish

1. Wash and boil potatoes until tender. Cool and cube into bite-size pieces. Place potatoes into a bowl. Add onion, crumbled bacon and cheese.
2. In a separate mixing bowl, combine the sour cream and mayonnaise. Add garlic powder, steak seasoning, Tabasco and Worcestershire and whisk together. You want it to be a little on the salty side since it's got to work with the potatoes. Tweak seasonings as needed.
3. Add half of your dressing to the potato mixture and gently give it a good mix. Then add half of what is left of the dressing and mix again. Does it look like the potatoes have enough dressing? If so, then don't add the rest, but if it's on the dry side for your taste, add the remainder of the dressing.
4. Top with diced chives and refrigerate prior to serving.

Throwed Rolls
Recipe from the St. Louis Post-Dispatch, *June 1991. It was noted in the paper that this recipe was tested "to adapt it to home kitchens," and it's noted to serve rolls "when they are cool enough to throw," so it's likely pretty close to the real deal found at the three Lambert's Café locations.*

1 teaspoon plus ¼ cup granulated sugar, divided
1 package dry active yeast

1 cup warm milk
¼ cup melted butter
1 egg, room temperature, beaten
1 teaspoon salt
4 cups all-purpose flour, divided
Vegetable oil (to oil bowl)

1. Stir 1 teaspoon sugar and yeast into ¼ cup tepid water (105 to 110 degrees F). Let stand 5 to 10 minutes until yeast begins to foam.
2. Thoroughly mix milk, butter, remaining ¼ cup sugar, egg and salt in a large bowl. Stir in yeast mixture and 3½ cups flour.
3. Turn dough out onto floured board; let dough rest while you clean and oil mixing bowl.
4. Knead dough gently for 5 minutes, working in as much of remaining ½ cup flour as needed, until dough is smooth and silky.
5. Return dough to bowl; cover with dry tea towel. Let rise in warm place until doubled in size.
6. Grease a 12-cup muffin tin.
7. Punch down dough. Pinch off pieces about 1½ inches in diameter (enough to fill one half of muffin cup) and roll into smooth balls. Place 2 balls in each prepared muffin cup. Note that it will be a tight fit.
8. Let rolls rise in warm place at least 30 minutes. Preheat oven to 350 degrees F. Bake rolls for 20 to 25 minutes or until light brown. Serve as soon as they are cool enough to throw. Yields 12 rolls.

Lambert's Fried Okra
Recipe from *Springfield News-Leader,* March 2000

6 cups fresh garden-grown cut okra
1 cup flour
1 cup breadcrumbs
¼ cup cornmeal
8 eggs, beaten
Vegetable oil for frying

1. Mix dry ingredients together.
2. Dip cut okra into egg batter, then roll in dry mixture.
3. Fry breaded okra in 350-degree vegetable oil until golden brown. Serve hot. Serves 12 people.

Pioneer Chili

Recipe from St. James Winery, which opened in 1970. The town of St. James is located on Route 66 and has a handful of route landmarks. This recipe includes the award-winning Pioneer Red wine, a red blend of Chambourcin, Norton and Rougeon grapes created to honor winery founders Jim and Pat Hofherr.

1 small white onion, chopped
1 green bell pepper, chopped
1 tablespoon olive oil
1 ½ pounds lean ground beef
1 tablespoon garlic, minced
1 (1 ¼-ounce) package dry chili seasoning mix
2 tablespoons chili powder
½ teaspoon cumin
½ teaspoon crushed red pepper flakes
1 (16-ounce) can diced tomatoes
1 (16-ounce) can ranch-style pinto beans
1 (16-ounce) can kidney beans, rinsed
2 cups Pioneer Red wine

1. Sauté onions and bell peppers in olive oil until tender.
2. Add ground beef and brown slowly over low heat, stirring often.
3. Add garlic and cook until ground beef is thoroughly cooked.
4. Add chili seasonings, chili powder, cumin, crushed red pepper, tomatoes, both beans and the wine.
5. Bring to a boil, then reduce heat and simmer for 3 hours.
6. After 3 hours, taste and add salt and pepper. Add sugar if needed to round out flavor. Makes 6 to 8 servings. Best served with a dollop of sour cream and shredded cheddar cheese.

Ott's Glazed Chicken Wings
Recipe from Ott Foods

4 tablespoons grape jelly
4 tablespoons Ott's Famous "The Red" Dressing
1 tablespoon prepared mustard
25 chicken wings

1. Preheat oven to 350 degrees F.
2. Combine grape jelly, dressing and mustard in a small saucepan. Heat thoroughly to create the glaze.
3. Arrange wings on a sheet pan. Brush liberally with glaze and bake for 20 to 30 minutes.
4. Remove finished wings to a serving platter and pour remaining glaze over them.

Copperhead Cocktail
Recipe from Copper Run Distillery in Walnut Shade, Missouri. The distillery, which opened in 2009, claims to be the first legal distillery in the Ozarks since the end of Prohibition. Spirits made here include bourbon, whiskey, white and spiced rums and moonshine. Walnut Shade is ten miles northeast of Branson.

1 ½ ounces Copper Run Overproof White Rum
1 ounce lime juice
1 ounce lemon juice
2 ounces grenadine or cranberry-pomegranate syrup
3 ounces club soda
Lemon wedge

In a shaker, combine rum, lime juice, lemon juice and grenadine. Pour over ice in a highball glass and top off with club soda. Garnish with a lemon wedge.

The Parkmoor Drive-In Onion Rings

Recipe courtesy of Frank Romano at the Parkmoor. Many St. Louis residents remember the original Parkmoor chain that was started by Lou McGinley in 1930. The King Burger, the Chickburger and the onion rings were among the favorite menu items. Although the original restaurant closed in 1999, the Parkmoor Drive-In opened in July 2020 in Webster Groves with onion rings and other favorites on the menu.

1 egg, beaten
1 cup beer
2 cups all-purpose flour
2 teaspoons dried parsley
2 teaspoons garlic powder
2 teaspoons dried oregano
1 cup oil for frying
3 large onions, sliced into rings

The famous onion rings from the Parkmoor Drive-In. *Frank Romano/Parkmoor Drive-In.*

1. Mix wet and dry ingredients separately.
2. Add dry to the wet and whisk until smooth. Look for the consistency of a pancake batter.
3. Heat oil in a deep frying pan to 350 degrees F (check using a candy thermometer).
4. Dredge the sliced onions through the batter and fry in heated oil. Make sure not to overcrowd the pan. Onion rings are done when they are golden brown.
5. Remove cooked onion rings from pan and place on a paper towel–lined platter to absorb excess oil. Serve with your favorite dipping sauce.

Chapter 5

PEACE, PROSPERITY AND
REDISCOVERING OUR PAST

T he headline filled the front page of the *St. Louis Globe-Democrat*, although it contained just two words: "Germany Surrenders." It was the morning of May 8, 1945, and Missouri's own President Harry Truman was set to proclaim V-E Day in a radio announcement at 8:00 a.m. that would be broadcast by four local stations. Bells rang as churches opened to give thanks. Schools and taverns closed as St. Louis was preparing to lift a brownout for that evening, allowing windows to glow once more at dusk. Similar celebrations were happening across the state as Missouri celebrated with the rest of the country. The Allies' victory in the Pacific was celebrated in August that same year, and with the close of World War II, Americans were ready for peace and prosperity.

The end of the war also affected what and how we ate. Service men and women returned home from overseas, their palates expanded. With war rationing a thing of the past and more Americans moving into the suburbs, outdoor grilling and patio barbecues became popular.

Companies grabbed on to this prosperity to market appliances, food items and product cookbooks to consumers. Convenience was another factor that steered food trends. During the war, many women got their first taste of working outside the home and continued to earn money in postwar years. Electric ranges and convenience appliances were marketed to working women. A Kansas City company, Rival Manufacturing, bought a nearly forgotten device, the Naxon Beanery, from its inventor, Irving Naxon, when he retired. Rebranded and refined, the beanery became the Crock-Pot.

While processed foods made lives easier, they weren't always the healthy choice, and we saw a food trend with an odd name emerge that would later become a lifestyle for many: farm-to-table (or farm-to-fork). A decade later, Missourians saw a resurgence in craft breweries and local wineries.

NORTHEAST MISSOURI

Pork steaks are as much a part of a St. Louis summer as the city's beloved Cardinals baseball team. But unlike the Cardinals, the pork steak didn't originate in St. Louis. However, a local grocery chain (Schnuck Markets) in the 1950s cut these thick pork blade steaks and advertised them for backyard barbecues.

No matter who cut the first pork steak, it remains a St. Louis favorite. More than 4 million pounds of pork steaks were purchased in a year, according to an article in the *Riverfront Times*. It's a personal preference to either cook the steaks entirely on the grill or to finish by baking the meat in sauce. But the end result should be tender pork slathered in a sweet tomato-based barbecue sauce. Pork steak purists insist on Maull's barbecue sauce, which was created in the 1920s in downtown St. Louis. Although no longer family owned, the sauce still is manufactured in the city.

What do you get when you accidentally drop a ravioli into hot oil instead of hot water? You'll have inadvertently created one of the most iconic dishes in St. Louis: toasted ravioli.

In the late 1940s, this delicious mistake happened in the Italian neighborhood known as the Hill. One story places the mishap at the long-gone Oldani's Restaurant, now the site of Mama's on the Hill. But another traces the dish to what's now Charlie Gitto's on the Hill, which was Angelo's Pasta House back in the day. The contemporary version of the dish coats the raviolis in breadcrumbs before frying and serving with red sauce.

St. Louis–style pizza is another local square-shaped delicacy, but this one can spark spirited debates. First, there's that cracker-thin crust. Then there are the square cuts with toppings going from edge to edge. Finally, Provel cheese continues to spark heated discussions, but if you're a St. Louisan, you just laugh while munching on a slice of hot square pizza.

Of course, square pizza wasn't invented in Missouri; this style of pizza is common throughout Italy and Sicily. What St. Louis added to square pizza was Provel, a processed cheese that combines white cheddar, Swiss and provolone cheeses with a touch of smoky flavoring. Stories vary as to the origin of this local delicacy—some point to the J.S. Hoffman Company, a Chicago-based maker of natural and processed cheeses as the patent holder, and other stories say that Costa Grocery in St. Louis came up with the idea to make a cheese that could melt like mozzarella but without the intense cheese pull.

But most local stories name Amedeo Fiore as the pioneer of St. Louis–style pizza. According to St. Louis restaurant historian and radiologist Harley Hammerman (https://www.losttables.com), Fiore and his wife, Elizabeth, moved to the city in the mid- to late 1930s and opened Melrose Café in 1945. Fiore, who cut his pizza into squares with scissors, eventually relocated the business, renamed Melrose Pizzeria, to a bigger location in north St. Louis County. The couple's son, Amedo Fiore Jr., operated the restaurant following his parents' retirement until 1977.

Probably few St. Louisans would argue that it was the pizza chain Imo's that popularized St. Louis–style pizza and Provel. Ed and Margie Imo opened a pizzeria on the Hill in 1964. Family members delivered the pizzas. The company today has more than one hundred stores and franchises in Missouri, Illinois and Kansas.

While Imo's was gaining its foothold in south St. Louis, about ninety minutes west of the city, a farming family was making plans to resurrect one of the state's earliest wineries. Jim and Betty Held purchased Stone Hill Winery from Bill Harrison in 1965. A year later, in Augusta, Lucian and Eva Dressel reopened Mount Pleasant Winery (now Mount Pleasant Estates). In 1980, Augusta became the country's first federally recognized American Viticultural Area (AVA) in the country—California's Napa Valley received its AVA designation one year later.

In total, Missouri has 130 wineries and 11 wine trails to discover. In 2021, David Hoffmann—a Washington, Missouri native—announced a $100 million development plan for Augusta that includes a sixty-room hotel, an upscale restaurant and a nine-hole golf course. Owner of the Hoffmann Family of Companies, Hoffmann has purchased Augusta Winery, Balducci Vineyards, Montelle Winery and Mount Pleasant Estates as part of the development that will be the Napa Valley of the Midwest, according to a company press release.

With Missouri's wine industry making a comeback, the craft brewing business was finding a home in St. Louis in the early 1990s, beginning with Schlafly (1991) and Morgan Street Brewing Company (1995). By 2017, according to the St. Louis Brewers Heritage Foundation, sixty microbreweries were either planned or in operation.

Another microbrewery, this one making root beer, brought back a St. Louis favorite in 1993. Fitz's root beer has a history stretching back to the 1930s, when the soda was served at Fitz's Famous Kitchenburgers, which was a small drive-in restaurant in Richmond Heights, a suburb of St. Louis. When the restaurant closed in 1976, owner Phil O'Brien took the recipe with him. Actually, the root beer went out of production around 1974, when the machinery used to make the soda broke down.

But today's version of Fitz's uses a recipe from 1947 and is bottled at the location on Delmar Avenue using a refurbished bottling line from the 1940s. In addition to root beer, Fitz's makes black cherry, Cardinal cream, original cream, vanilla mint, orange and orange cream, Key lime, grape and a new flavor, Shirley Temple. In 2019, Fitz's opened another restaurant in south St. Louis County.

In another sweet success story, Chocolate Chocolate Chocolate Company owner Dan Abel Sr. and his family have built a candy empire in St. Louis. While in college, Abel worked at a candy business, the Yum Yum Tree, and eventually set up a franchised store in St. Louis on Chippewa Street in 1981. When the Yum Yum Tree's founder passed away, Abel and his wife, Rosalie, purchased the business. The name was changed to Chocolate Chocolate Chocolate Company.

In addition to relaunching the beloved Mavrakos brand of chocolate in 2009 that had been popular in St. Louis, the Abel family purchased Bissinger's chocolate company in 2019. There are five Chocolate Chocolate Chocolate Company locations in St. Louis and St. Charles, Missouri, including the factory in the Hill.

A local focus on food was also gaining steam in the 1990s in Missouri. Slow Food USA, with chapters in St. Louis and Kansas City, was founded in 1989 to "reconnect Americans with people, traditions, plants, animals, social, and waters that produce our food." In a recent webinar sponsored by SlowFood Saint Louis, Rob Connoley, chef at Bulrush restaurant, said that most ingredients used in the restaurant are locally sourced, with the exception of sugar and salt. "We do it to support local farmers and economy, but it's also about biodiversity. I want to educate people why we cook this way; it's not just a trendy thing," he said. For Connoley, it's about authenticity, history and truth.

The menu at his restaurant is "rooted in Ozark cuisine," but Connoley simplifies the description as food many of us were raised on. By researching family journals and letters from the 1800s, he's uncovered a cuisine that explores different traditions.

"Most people think Ozark cuisine is wild game like possum, raccoon and squirrel, and that's part of it, but it's looking at food cultures of Osage nation, enslaved people, and settlers who mainly migrated to Missouri's Ozarks from Appalachia. As a restaurant, we're exploring each of them," he said.

Northwest Missouri

Walking through the door at Christopher Elbow Chocolate in Kansas City's Crossroads District is a pivotal moment for any chocolate lover. The chocolates on display look like jewelry. *Food & Wine* recently named Elbow one of the top fifty chocolate makers in the country.

Originally a pastry chef, Elbow taught himself how to make beautiful things out of chocolate. Customers started to ask about the wonderful chocolate candy. In 2003, Elbow began to make his artisanal chocolates for mail-order and small wholesale business. His retail shop in Kansas City opened in 2007, and he later opened his chocolate boutique in San Francisco.

"Every day, every batch we make, we pay attention to all the detail so they come out perfect," Elbow said. He added they never put out anything—even as samples—that are not perfect. A batch may consist of 900 to 1,200 pieces, each enrobed by hand.

Another pastry chef and confiseur (chocolate maker), André Bollier, had a dream to bring fine European chocolates and baked confections to the United States. In June 1955, André and his wife, Elsbeth, emigrated from Switzerland to the Midwest, and by October, he had opened his shop. But according to grandson René Bollier, the Midwest palate didn't demand pastries and chocolates made with pure butter, whipped cream and natural flavors and ingredients.

André went on to open a tearoom serving light Swiss luncheons, hoping that would draw more people in, who in turn would purchase candies and pastries to take home. When the demand for chocolate took an upswing in the 1970s, sales at André's exploded, and son Marcel and his wife, Connie, joined André's in 1974 to spearhead the expansion of the chocolate department. Marcel and Connie's son, René, and his wife, Nancy, came on board in 2001, marking the third generation to work in the business. In addition to the original location on Main Street in Kansas City, André's Rivaz in Overland Park, Kansas, also offers a tearoom and retail shop.

The barbecue scene continued to grow in postwar years. In 1957, Russ Fiorella opened a small barbecue business in Kansas City. His eldest son,

A selection of Kansas City's award-winning chocolate made by Christopher Elbow. *Visit KC.*

Jack, worked alongside his father until 1974, when he branched off to open Fiorella's Jack Stack in the neighborhood of Martin City, which sits on the Missouri-Kansas border. Today, this popular local chain, still family owned, has five Kansas City locations, plus a catering division, and also ships its barbecue nationwide.

Another family barbecue business got its start in the 1970s. Leavy B. Jones, owner of Jones Bar-B-Q, taught his daughters Deborah ("Little") and Mary ("Shorty") all he knew about smoking meats and running a business. With more than thirty years of experience, the sisters are two of just a handful of female pit masters in the region and now run the family business in Kansas City, Kansas. The family's secret sauce is bottled and sold.

It was friends, not family, who brought Jeff and Joy Stehney into the barbecue circle. In 1990, the Stehneys attended their first barbecue contest with their friends. Soon after, they formed a competition team called Slaughterhouse Five and began to rack up awards. They and a partner launched a catering business in 1995. One year later, a Kansas City location near the Stehneys' home opened up. The couple bought out their partner and in 1997 opened Joe's Kansas City Bar-B-Que. In addition to the original spot in a gas station, there are locations in Olathe and Leawood, Kansas, plus an event center.

The entire country would have a small taste of Kansas City thanks to Rich Davis, who developed the sauce in 1978 that came to be known as KC Masterpiece. Davis, a psychiatrist by trade, concocted his sauce—originally known as K.C. Soul Style BBQ—and sold it out of his personal vehicle. In 1980, the sauce won big at the annual American Royal competition, and that lit the fires of demand. Davis sold his business in 1986 to the Kingsford Product Company.

The thick molasses-and-tomato-based original KC Masterpiece sauce at one time was synonymous with Kansas City–style barbecue, but Carolyn Wells, cofounder of the Kansas City Barbeque Society, said "a little heat, a little sweet, a touch of vinegar and spices make for a good representation of finishing sauce in the Melting Pot of BBQ."

Of course, there's more to Kansas City food than barbecue, and another iconic dish can be found in the neighborhood of Columbus Park. Chicken Spiedini is the signature dish at Garozzo's Italian restaurant. Noted on the restaurant's site as "a Garozzo's creation," the chicken is marinated and rolled in Italian breadcrumbs, skewered and grilled. It's finished and presented in several ways, but the amogio sauce—olive oil, lemon juice, garlic and herbs—is the most popular.

Michael Garozzo, born and raised in St. Louis, worked in restaurants starting as a busboy, dreaming of having his own place one day. In 1989, he opened the first Garozzo's location in Columbus Park. While the Chicken Spiedini here is outstanding and the restaurant has over the years attracted a number of celebrity patrons and garnered numerous awards, it's doubtful that Garozzo was the first to think of using chicken in a spiedini recipe. A dish called spiedie—marinated chunks of meat on skewers—was popular in Upstate New York in the 1930s. As early as 1987, a chicken spiedini, described as breaded breast of chicken skewered and basted with lemon garlic sauce, was part of the menu at Saputo's Caffe Italia, which has since closed.

Kansas City's craft cocktail scene is as varied and exciting as its food. Bartender Ryan Maybee was one of the first to showcase craft cocktails in his small speakeasy, Manifesto, which opened in 2009 in the Crossroads Arts District. Although it has since closed, there are a number of bars and craft distilling companies in the city where patrons can sip outstanding, handcrafted cocktails. The Monarch, SoT (South of Truman) and Julep

Boulevard Brewing Company's campus in Kansas City. *Visit KC.*

Cocktail Club are trendy and recommended places to try. Distilleries in and around Kansas City include J. Rieger, Tom's Town, S.D. Strong, Restless Spirits, Lifted Spirits and Mean Mule.

Boulevard Brewing Company, established in 1989, has grown to become Kansas City's biggest artisan brewer, but a blog that's just about Kansas City beer also lists nearly forty craft breweries in the area.

A day trip out of the city to the charming town of Weston, Missouri, has opportunities for food and wine lovers. Stop at Green Dirt Farm, home of some incredible sheep's milk cheeses. Founder Sarah Hoffman in 2002 started this humane, sustainable sheep dairy.

Pirtle Winery opened its doors (in a former Weston church that dates to the mid-1800s) in 1978. It bottles red, white and fruit wines, as well as a collection of meads (honey wine), some infused with berries.

Southwest Missouri

Yin Wing Leong emigrated from China to the United States when he was nineteen years old with the plan to earn enough money to bring his wife and baby son to America. But World War II changed his plans, separating him from his young family for several years.

Still, he went on to serve in the U.S. Army. While training, his drill sergeant pinned the name David on him because he couldn't pronounce his given name.

Following a tour in the army, David was working in a Florida restaurant when a surgeon visiting from Springfield, Missouri, tasted and enjoyed David's food. The doctor made him an offer to be head chef at his restaurant, the Lotus Garden, in Springfield, and he accepted.

Eventually, David had saved enough money to open his own restaurant, Leong's Tea House, in 1963. But days before its scheduled opening, vandals bombed the building. The family fought off this attack, and the restaurant opened and built a following.

Yet David sensed that the restaurant's authentic Cantonese cuisine needed something else to appeal to the Ozark palate. He tweaked his cashew chicken stir fry recipe to include fried chicken and a salty oyster sauce–based gravy. Springfield-style cashew chicken became a big hit and was served at Leong's Tea House until it closed in 1997.

One of David's children, Wing Yee Leong, who is also a chef in his own right, joined his father to open Leong's Asian Diner in 2010, with Wing Yee as the executive chef. His father passed away in 2020 at the age of ninety-nine, but Springfield-style cashew chicken now is served across the United States.

Another family created a frozen dessert that has been a part of Springfield summers for more than forty years. In 1974, Dan Fortner's treat, Pineapple Whip, was available at the Ozark Empire Fair, but after several years, customers urged the family to make it available beyond the days the fair was held each year.

Fortner and sons Mike and Chris set up a trailer in 1986 on the Westlake Hardware parking lot on south Campbell in Springfield. A few years after that, more locations were built, and today, Springfield has three Pineapple Whip locations. The family doesn't share the Pineapple Whip recipe, but in addition to original pineapple, other flavors include grape, strawberry-kiwi and lemon-berry.

More sweets are found on East Commercial Street in Springfield. Chocolate lovers know that the single-origin bars made by Shawn Askinosie and his crew can be found here. Some of the finest bean-to-bar chocolate is made in this small factory, which opened in 2007.

In the 1990s, Askinosie was working as a criminal defense lawyer, burning out from the high-pressure job. To help with stress, he found baking, the path that led him to learn more about chocolate. He traveled to Ecuador in 2005 to learn how chocolate is harvested and made, and a year later, he bought a building for his chocolate factory. Askinosie trades fairly and directly with global growers for his beans, which are then roasted and made into bars at the factory.

In the Branson area, the Keeter Center's Dobyns Dining Room at the College of the Ozarks does farm-to-fork menus with products produced by students. In addition to an on-campus dairy, students run farms and produce smoked meats as part of the 120 student work opportunities. Some of the students are working toward a degree in the culinary or hospitality industries, but all put in fifteen hours each week to help pay for their tuition. The dining room serves lunch and dinner Thursday through Saturday and brunch on Sunday.

Gardeners may be familiar with Baker Creek Heirloom Seed Company in Mansfield, Missouri. Started in 1998 by owner Jere Gettle as a hobby, Baker Creek has become one of the largest sellers of rare heirloom seeds. The site, which includes a seed store and a pioneer village, is open weekdays.

Southeast Missouri

Linda Williams like to dish about dirt. As a master gardener and the owner of Windrush Farm Arts & Plants in Farmington, Missouri, she knows the importance of healthy, organic soil. To that end, she creates her own potting soil in which she grows her various plants at the farm. She starts her seeds in either peat moss or vermiculite and then transplants the seedlings into her organic potting mix.

"When I first started gardening, I bought the premade bags of potting soil, and it was okay. But as I began to make conscious choices about the way that I wanted to garden, I realized that I wanted to make my own potting soil so that I could have some control over what I was growing my plants in. The recipe that I use has evolved over the years, and some years it's tweaked according to the ingredients that I have available," Williams said.

She bought the Farmington property in 1997. Williams said that it needed a lot of work, but her intent was to create a quiet refuge in which to live. Although she had no previous gardening or farming background at the time, Williams said that she was concerned about how humans were treating our planet and read a lot about sustainable agriculture. She enrolled in a master gardener program through the University of Missouri Extension and went on to conduct workshops and teach continuing education classes at the Mineral Area College.

Her brother, Leonard Williams (who lives with her on the farm), in 2020 built a produce stand that she said is "on the honor system, socially distanced, unless the customer wants help" and features vegetable, herb and flower plants grown at Windrush. Williams also sells fresh bouquets and farm-created decorative art objects, as well as "soil food," an alfalfa-based amendment that she said is good for tired soil. In 2021, she introduced three varieties of hybrid tomatoes developed especially for growing in planters.

"I would like everyone to understand that sustainable agriculture uses the earth in a way that is environmentally safe, economically viable and socially just," Williams said. "It's not enough to 'buy organic.' The soil life must be nurtured. The workers must be able to work in humane conditions and be able to comfortably feed, clothe and house their families. The farmer must be able to produce [crops] every year without fear of crippling debt and climate change."

While in Farmington, visit a few Missouri wineries, like Sand Creek Vineyards and Twin Oaks Vineyard and Winery. Both are family-owned; Sand Creek opened in 2002, and Twin Oaks—named for the four-hundred-year-old oak trees on the property—opened about four years later.

On the popular Route du Vin Wine Trail from Ste. Geneviève to Farmington, oenophiles will discover a variety of wineries, from large commercial enterprises to quaint family-owned businesses. The trail is part of the vast Ozark Mountain American Viticultural Area (AVA), which covers 3.5 million acres in southern Missouri extending into Arkansas and Oklahoma. In Ste. Geneviève, Chaumette and Crown Valley are the

Chaumette Winery in Ste. Geneviève has a beautiful patio with outstanding views. *Ste. Geneviève Tourism.*

biggest and perhaps most widely known wineries along the trail, but there are others definitely worth visiting. Cave Vineyard Winery & Distillery in Ste. Geneviève is family owned and opened in 2004. Patrons enjoy wine and food purchases inside a natural saltpeter cave underneath the winery's tasting room. There's also a biscotti bar, and a small-batch brandy was launched in 2021.

Charleville Vineyards, also in Ste. Geneviève, is a family-owned winery that opened in 2003. The site includes a refurbished 1860 log cabin that's available for overnight guests. Try a pizza baked in the brick oven.

CENTRAL MISSOURI

Farmers' markets aren't new—the markets at Kansas City and St. Louis, for example, started in the nineteenth century. Markets are found in cities of various sizes throughout the state, but the Agricultural Park in Columbia not only serves as the permanent home for the award-winning market, but it also names as its mission to help residents get healthy local food and spend time outdoors while connecting people to sustainable agriculture.

Columbia's Agricultural Park—located within the city's Clary-Shy Community Park—opened its first phase in 2019 that included the MU Health Pavilion (the market's new home), urban farm plots, demonstration gardens, a playground, trails and plenty of parking. Phase II, which is targeted for completion in 2022, will include a kitchen and event center. A private-public partnership called Friends of the Farm includes the Columbia Farmers' Market and its Sustainable Farms and Communities, which helps bring healthy food to low-income families; the Columbia Center for Urban Agriculture, which will eventually make its home at the Agricultural Park; and the Columbia Department of Parks and Recreation.

Corrina Smith, executive director for the Columbia Farmers' Market, said that sixty-five vendors are present on average at the Saturday market, which is held throughout the year. In addition, a Tuesday morning and Thursday afternoon market is offered summer through fall.

The producer-only market, which celebrated its fortieth anniversary in 2020, was also awarded the Mayor's Climate Protection Agreement Award. Although the market uses less packaging and encourages shoppers to bring reusable bags, the biggest way it helps reduce carbon footprint is the shorter distance from farms to the market, according to Smith. She said that on average, the food sold at grocery chains travels 1,500 miles from the farm to the store, but all vendors at Columbia's markets come no more than 50 miles. Shopping from local farms helps local economies, she added. "When you make a grocery store purchase, 15 cents [on a dollar] goes back to the farmer. But when you buy direct from that farmer, they're getting that entire dollar," Smith said.

One of the local farmers featured at the market, Lage Farms near Jefferson City, specializes in Wagyu beef. The Barred Owl Butcher & Table in Columbia also sells Lage Farms beef and has been a vendor at the market. The Barred Owl, which opened in 2016, specializes in whole-animal butchery and charcuterie. The retail side also sells artisan cheeses and baked goods. The restaurant features local and seasonal ingredients.

Since 2005, Sycamore Restaurant has served innovative American fare using local products. It's a favorite of Columbia's residents and visitors who also appreciate Sycamore's eclectic wine list, craft brews and cocktails.

A small downtown market, Root Cellar, offers sustainable products and produce grown by family farms. Root Cellar has been a part of Columbia's downtown since 2001, and Chelsea and Jake Davis bought the business in 2011. The market is open for trade, although there's a waiting list for the food subscription delivery service.

Recipes

Speedy Pork Steak with Grilled Greens

Recipe courtesy Schnuck Markets. In St. Louis, it's not summer without a pork steak on the grill, and this dish is ready in about 30 minutes, leaving plenty of time for backyard fun.

4 pork steaks, about ½-inch thick
2 tablespoons olive oil
Salt and pepper
Barbecue sauce, your favorite
1 bunch kale or mustard greens
Lemon juice

1. Prepare grill for two-zone cooking—one for pork steaks and one for greens.
2. Coat pork steaks with olive oil and season with salt and pepper.
3. Add pork to grill over direct heat and cook until internal temperature comes to 145 degrees F (6 to 8 minutes). Flip once halfway through. Add

2 minutes before pork is done. Brush liberally with barbecue sauce and cook 1 minute per side.

4. Drizzle 1 tablespoon olive oil over greens. Grill over indirect heat until greens start to char, about 1 to 2 minutes. Remove from grill and chop into pieces; season with lemon juice, salt and pepper. Makes 4 to 6 servings.

Toasted Ravioli

Recipe from the Pasta House Company, originally published in *Food Editors' Hometown Favorites Cookbook: American Regional and Local Specialties.*

Frozen ravioli, homemade or store-bought
Milk
Dry breadcrumbs
Vegetable oil for deep-frying
Grated Parmesan cheese

1. Remove ravioli from freezer. Do not brush off flour.
2. Pour milk into a small dish.
3. Place breadcrumbs in a small dish.
4. Heat oil to 375 degrees F.
5. Dip frozen ravioli in milk, then roll in breadcrumbs. Fry in oil about 3 to 4 minutes or until golden brown. (Ravioli will sink at first and then rise to top of oil when done.) Turn squares to promote even cooking. Remove from oil and drain well. While hot, sprinkle with Parmesan. Serve with red sauce.

Quick and Easy Pasta Sauce

Recipe featured in the St. Louis Post-Dispatch, *December 1998, as part of a story about* Fare to Remember, *a cookbook project by the Assistance League of St. Louis. The sauce can be served with the toasted ravioli.*

2 tablespoons olive oil
1 large onion, chopped

3 cloves garlic, minced
¾ pound lean ground beef
1 (28-ounce) can plum tomatoes
1 (6-ounce) can tomato paste
1 tablespoon dried basil
½ teaspoon granulated sugar
Salt to taste
½ teaspoon ground pepper

1. Heat oil in large skillet. Add onion and cook until translucent. Add garlic and cook briefly (about 1 minute).
2. Add ground beef and cook, stirring to break into small pieces, until there is no more pink in meat.
3. Add tomatoes (crush by hand or spoon), tomato paste, basil, sugar, salt and pepper. Stir to combine.
4. Simmer, uncovered, for about 30 minutes. Serve as dipping sauce for toasted ravioli or with pasta. Yields 5 cups.

Budweiser and Provel Cheese Dip

Recipe from Schnuck Markets. Two St. Louis classics come together in an easy dip that's perfect for a backyard gathering or to enjoy while watching the Cardinals play ball.

2 tablespoons butter
1 pound Imo's® branded Provel cheese
¼ cup Budweiser
¼ cup milk
1 teaspoon Dijon mustard
½ teaspoon garlic powder
½ teaspoon onion powder
¼ teaspoon cayenne pepper

1. Melt butter in a medium pan over medium-high heat.
2. Add remaining ingredients to pan. Continue to cook, stirring constantly, until combined and melted (about 8 minutes). Serve warm.

Easy Peach Vignoles Trifle

Recipe courtesy Missouri Wine and Grape Board. Vignoles is a popular white wine in Missouri. This dessert is delicious immediately, or it can be made up to a day ahead of time and kept covered in the refrigerator.

1 ½ cups Missouri Vignoles wine
¼ cup granulated sugar
5 large peaches
1 package instant French vanilla pudding
2 cups milk
2 cups heavy whipping cream
2 teaspoons pure vanilla extract
4 tablespoons powdered sugar
Pound cake (if using frozen, thaw before making trifle)

1. In a medium saucepan, bring wine and sugar to a low boil and simmer until the liquid is reduced by half, about 10 to 12 minutes. Let cool when finished.
2. While the wine is simmering, prepare your other layer components. If you prefer your peaches skinless, wash them and cut a shallow "X" in the bottom. Submerge peaches in boiling water for 1 minute. Carefully remove

Fresh peaches and Missouri Vignoles white wine are the star ingredients in this trifle. *Missouri Grape and Wine Board.*

from the boiling water and put peaches directly into a bowl of ice water. Once they've cooled, the skins will slide right off. If you don't mind the skin on your peaches, skip this step and go right to removing the pit and chopping the fruit into bite-size pieces.

3. In a large bowl, prepare the French vanilla pudding with milk according to package instructions. Cut pound cake into 1-inch cubes.

4. In a medium bowl, beat cream, vanilla extract and powdered sugar until stiff peaks form. Fold half of the whipped cream into the pudding just until mixed.

5. When the Vignoles syrup is cool, stir it into the peaches.

6. Begin building your trifle. Make a full layer of pound cake, top with peaches and then add a layer of pudding mixture. Repeat in the same order. Spoon or pipe the remaining whipped cream on top to finish it off. Makes 12 to 16 servings.

Acorn Financiers (Brown Butter Breads)

Recipe courtesy of Chef Rob Connoley of Bulrush, who noted that baking at high heat initially creates the domed, cracked effect on muffins. Connoley, a James Beard semifinalist chef, ensures that all ingredients are locally sourced from small farmers or made or foraged by restaurant employees. While Connoley makes his own acorn flour, he noted that it can be found in some Asian markets or online.

¾ cup unsalted butter
⅔ cup sugar
¾ cup acorn flour
¼ cup almond flour
1 cup cake flour
2 teaspoons baking powder
7 egg whites

1. Preheat oven to 425 degrees F. Grease 12 muffin tins with extra butter.

2. Melt ¾ cup butter over medium-high heat. Turn heat down to medium and continue cooking until it starts to turn brown. Remove from heat and allow to cool.

3. In a mixing bowl, add dry ingredients and mix with whisk.

Acorn Financiers feature acorn and almond flours. *Deborah Reinhardt.*

4. In a separate bowl, add egg whites and sugar and beat with whisk until eggs just start to turn frothy. Slowly add the cooled butter to the egg and sugar mixture and mix well.

5. Using a rubber spatula or wooden spoon, add the wet ingredients to the mixing bowl with dry ingredients. The batter should resemble cupcake batter. If desired, add a good pinch of salt and stir.

6. Fill each muffin tin about ¾ full. An ice cream scoop works well here. Gently tap the muffin pan on counter, place on a baking tray and place on middle rack of oven. Bake for 6 minutes.

7. Turn oven down to 375 degrees and bake another 6 to 8 minutes; when toothpick comes out clean, the financiers are done. Set on rack and allow to cool about 5 minutes before turning out onto a plate or board. Makes 12 muffins.

❖ ❖ ❖

Levee High Apple Pie

Recipe from The Blue Owl® Bakery and Restaurant in Kimmswick, Missouri. Opened in 1985 by Mary Hostetter, The Blue Owl's best-selling pie was inspired by a 1993 Mississippi River flood that forced the restaurant's evacuation and threatened the historical town. Kimmswick is located off Interstate 55—stop in while traveling from St. Louis to the Rue du Vin Wine Trail in southeast Missouri.

12 cups (about 18) Golden Delicious apples, peeled and thinly sliced
1 cup plus 1 tablespoon sugar
¼ cup flour
2 teaspoons cinnamon
Dash of salt
2 deep-dish unbaked pie crusts
1 tablespoon butter
¼ cup milk
1 ½ cups melted caramels (21 ounces)
2 tablespoons evaporated milk
½ cup chopped pecans

Levee High Apple Pie packs in twelve cups of apples. *The Blue Owl Bakery.*

1. Combine apples, sugar, flour, cinnamon and salt. Mound filling by hand or use a small, deep mixing bowl for a mold. (The bakery uses a Tupperware lettuce crisper.)

2. Invert the filling into the bottom crust and dot with butter. Cover the mounded filling with top crust. Moisten, seal and flute edges tightly. Brush top crust with a small amount of milk and 1 tablespoon sugar mixed together. Prick crust to allow steam to vent.

3. Bake at 450 degrees F for 15 minutes, then reduce heat to 350 degrees and bake for 1 hour or until crust is golden brown.

4. For the topping, melt caramels in microwave. Add evaporated milk and stir until smooth. Add pecans and stir. Spread over pie starting at the base and working up. Makes 8 servings.

Chicken Spiedini/Spiedini con Pollo di Garozzo

Recipe courtesy of Visit KC, the tourism organization for Kansas City, Missouri.

4 boneless, skinless chicken breast halves
⅓ cup Italian seasoned breadcrumbs
⅓ cup grated Parmesan cheese
1 tablespoon chopped fresh parsley
2 teaspoons grated lemon zest
2 cloves minced garlic
2 tablespoons olive oil
2 tablespoons butter, melted

1. Place chicken between sheets of plastic wrap. Pound gently with mallet until chicken breasts are ⅛-inch thick.
2. On waxed paper, combine breadcrumbs, cheese, parsley, lemon zest and garlic.
3. In a shallow dish, combine oil and melted butter.
4. Dip chicken into butter and oil mixture and then coat with crumb mixture. Tightly roll up each breast and secure with toothpicks if needed.
5. Cut chicken into 1-inch-thick pieces. Thread on a metal skewer. Remove toothpicks. Repeat with remaining chicken breasts.
6. Place skewers on prepared grill over medium-hot coals. Cook for 5 minutes per side or until chicken is cooked through. Makes 4 servings.

Creamy Conchiglie (Shell) Pasta with Tomato and Zucchini

Recipe by Deborah Reinhardt. Green Dirt Farm's garlic and herb sheep milk cheese creates the sauce for this dish.

1 pound of medium shell pasta
2 tablespoons olive oil
1 small yellow onion, chopped
2 medium zucchinis, cut into 1-inch pieces
2 cloves garlic, minced
2 cups grape tomatoes sliced in half

Garlic and herb sheep cheese from Green Dirt Farm gives Creamy Conchiglie its satisfying tang. *Deborah Reinhardt.*

4 ounces fresh garlic and herb sheep milk spreadable cheese
2 tablespoons fresh lemon juice
Salt and pepper

1. In a large stockpot, bring about 5 quarts of water to a boil. Add 2 tablespoons of salt. Cook pasta al dente according to directions on box.
2. While pasta is cooking, turn stove to medium heat to preheat a large skillet. Add olive oil and onion. Cook onion until it starts to become translucent.
3. Add the zucchini and cook until it just starts to get some color. Add the garlic and stir vegetables well, cooking 1 additional minute.
4. Add the grape tomatoes and cook until they start to soften. Turn stove down to medium-low, turn off the pasta burner (do not drain) and add the sheep milk cheese to the skillet. Stir so cheese melts and coats the vegetables.
5. Using a straining ladle, transfer pasta into the skillet and toss well. Add lemon juice. If the sauce is too tight, add a bit of pasta water to the skillet and stir. Add salt and pepper to taste. Makes 6 servings.

Springfield Cashew Chicken
This recipe, courtesy of Leong's Asian Diner, was first published in 417 Magazine.

2 pounds chicken breast, diced into 1-inch pieces

For the flour mixture:
4 cups all-purpose flour
1 tablespoon seasoned salt (like Lawry's®)
1 teaspoon ground white pepper
2 tablespoon granulated garlic
½ teaspoon cayenne pepper (optional)

For the milk batter:
3 eggs
3 cups milk
1 tablespoon seasoned salt
½ teaspoon ground white pepper

For the cashew chicken sauce:
3½ cups chicken broth
½ teaspoon salt
½ teaspoon sugar
¼ cup soy sauce
2 tablespoons oyster sauce
1 pinch ground ginger
⅛ teaspoon sesame oil
¼ cup cornstarch
¼ cup water

For serving:
4 ounces cashew nuts
4 ounces chopped green onions

1. Heat fryer or oil to 350 degrees F.
2. Place all flour mixture ingredients in a medium bowl. Mix well.

139

Springfield Cashew Chicken from Leong's Asian Diner. *Springfield CVB.*

3. In another medium bowl, beat the eggs and then add milk, seasoned salt and white pepper. Mix well.
4. Place diced chicken into flour mixture, coating all sides, and then dip into the milk batter; place back into flour mixture, again coating all sides.
5. Place all breaded chicken pieces on a cookie sheet until ready to fry. Blanch chicken pieces in the heated fryer or oil until ¾ of the way cooked, approximately 2 to 3 minutes. Place partially cooked chicken on a paper towel–lined cookie sheet or on a wire rack to hold for service.
6. To make the cashew chicken sauce, mix together chicken broth, salt, sugar, soy sauce, oyster sauce, ginger and sesame oil and bring to a boil. Add the cornstarch to the water to make a slurry, then add your slurry to the boiling mixture and whisk constantly until you reach a gravy-like consistency.
7. When ready to serve, fry chicken a second time for 2 to 3 minutes. Top with cashew sauce, cashew nuts and green onions.

DIY Dole Whip

(If you can't get to Springfield, Missouri, for the iconic Pineapple Whip treat, this make-at-home dessert from Dole® fits the bill.)

1 cup ripe pineapple, chopped and frozen
1 banana, peeled and frozen
2½ teaspoons powdered sugar
½ cup unsweetened coconut milk
1 teaspoon lime juice

Combine all ingredients in a blender or food processor. Cover and blend until smooth, about 3 minutes. Garnish with fresh pineapple and serve immediately.

Polenta with Dehydrated Plum Tomatoes and Basil

Recipe courtesy of Linda Williams, Windrush Farm Arts & Plants in Farmington, Missouri

1 quart cold water
1 teaspoon salt
2 cups dehydrated Principe Borghese (or other cherry-sized) tomatoes
1 cup coarsely ground white or yellow cornmeal
1 teaspoon dried basil
2 tablespoons unsalted butter
1 cup grated Parmesan cheese

1. Pour water into a large (2-quart or larger) saucepan. Add salt and dehydrated tomatoes. Bring to a boil over medium heat.
2. Slowly add cornmeal, stirring constantly. When mixture returns to a boil, cover pan and reduce heat to medium-low. Cook, stirring occasionally, until mixture is very thick and the tomatoes are soft.
3. Stir in basil; turn the heat off and add the butter and grated cheese, mixing well.
4. Pour the mixture into a well-buttered metal baking pan (don't use a nonstick pan because it will get scratched). When the mixture is cooled (next day is

best), cut the polenta into squares and fry the squares in a small amount of butter or olive oil until brown on both sides.

5. Serve topped with pasta sauce or simply with a sprinkle of grated Parmesan cheese. This also makes a nice side dish, spooned hot right out of the pot. Makes 6 generous portions.

Eggplant Paté

Recipe courtesy of Mighty Acorn Farm, a vendor at the Columbia Farmers' Market. The dish utilizes slim Asian eggplants, which don't require peeling. The farm, owned by John Corn and Sandy Gummersheimer, is just north of Columbia.

3 to 4 fresh Asian eggplant, caps removed but otherwise whole
1 whole zucchini squash
1 medium onion
½ to 1 cup roasted cashews
3 cloves garlic
3 tablespoons olive oil
3 to 4 tablespoons soft goat cheese
Salt and pepper to taste
½ to 1 cup fresh basil

1. Steam all vegetables until soft. While hot, add to the blender.
2. Save some of the liquid depending on the consistency desired. Add the rest of the ingredients, incorporating the basil last.
3. Variations will include adding Parmesan cheese or roasting the vegetables instead of steaming. If roasting vegetables, add an extra half hour and some extra liquid. Makes 4 servings.

CONCLUSION

Missouri's story is best told through its food, giving us a chance to actually taste history. From the earliest indigenous people to the inventive chefs of today, Missourians have made the most of the state's bountiful agricultural resources. Along the way, the menu has been influenced by African and European cultures, and as more people from other countries continue to settle in Missouri, residents and visitors can sample a taste of the world without leaving the state. Missourians tackled westward expansion, weathered rough times (sometimes using whatever means and methods they had available) and managed to find ways to produce our food and drink with renewed ingenuity and equity. We still have more to learn, and this will make Missouri's table even more exciting.

TRAVELING THROUGH MISSOURI

It's impossible to include every notable historic site, maker, chef, restaurant, winery or brewery in the state. But now that your appetite has been stimulated, use this book as your map to help you to explore Missouri. The bibliography is also a good starting point to learn more about Missouri's foods.

Tourism organizations around Missouri are marvelous resources for food-loving travelers. Those listed here can help augment the stories told within this book with additional trip-planning information.

Arrow Rock, www.arrowrock.org, (660) 837-3608.

Augusta Chamber of Commerce, https://augusta-chamber.org/plan-your-visit, (636) 228-4005.

Bowling Green Convention & Visitors Bureau, https://visitbowlinggreenmo.com, (573) 324-3733.

Branson/Lakes Area Convention & Visitors Bureau, https://www.explorebranson.com, (800) 296-0463.

Cape Girardeau Convention & Visitors Bureau, https://www.visitcape.com, (800) 777-0068.

Columbia Convention and Visitors Bureau, https://www.visitcolumbiamo.com, (573) 874-2489.

Farmington Convention & Tourism Bureau, https://discoverfarmingtonmo.com, (573) 756-1701.

Gateway Arch, https://www.gatewayarch.com, (877) 982-1410.

Hannibal Convention & Visitors Bureau, https://www.visithannibal.com, (573) 221-2477.

Hermann Tourism, https://visithermann.com, (573) 789-0771.

Independence Department of Tourism, https://visitindependence.com, (800) 748-7323.

Jefferson City Convention and Visitors Bureau, https://www.visitjeffersoncity.com, (800) 769-4183.

Kansas City, https://www.visitkc.com, (800) 767-7700.

Lake of the Ozarks Convention & Visitors Bureau, https://www.funlake.com, (800) 386-5253.

Missouri Division of Tourism, https://www.visitmo.com, (573) 751-4133.

Missouri Grape and Wine Board, https://missouriwine.org.

Missouri State Parks, https://mostateparks.com.

Old Mines Area Historical Society, https://omahs.weebly.com.

Sikeston Convention & Visitors Bureau, https://www.sikeston.org/index_convention.php, (888) 309-6591.

Springfield Missouri Convention & Visitors Bureau, https://www.springfieldmo.org, (800) 678-8767.

St. Charles Convention and Visitors Bureau, https://www.discoverstcharles.com, (800) 366-2427.

St. Joseph Convention & Visitors Bureau, https://stjomo.com, (816) 232-1839.

St. Louis Convention & Visitors Commission, https://explorestlouis.com, (800) 916-8938.

Ste. Geneviève Department of Tourism, https://www.visitstegen.com, (800) 373-7007.

Ulysses S. Grant National Historic Site, https://www.nps.gov/ulsg/index.htm, (314) 842-1867.

Weston Chamber of Commerce, https://www.westonmo.com, (816) 640-2909.

BIBLIOGRAPHY

Chapter 1

Brackenridge, Henry M. *Reflections of the West*. N.p., 1834.

———. *Views of Louisiana, Together with a Journal of a Voyage up the Missouri River in 1811*. Pittsburgh, PA: Cramer, Spear and Eichbaum, 1814.

Braudel, Fernand. *Structures of Everyday Life*. Cambridge, UK: Cambridge University Press, 1982.

Corbett, Suzanne. Historical recipes and program materials for the National Park Service, Gateway Arch and Old Courthouse, 2000–2015.

Devoy, John. "A History of the City of St. Louis and Vicinity from the Earliest to the Present." In *The Compiler*. 1st ed. Salt Lake City, UT: digitized by Family Search International, 2019. Originally published St. Louis, MO, 1898.

Ekberg, Carl. *Colonial Ste. Geneviève: An Adventure on the Mississippi Frontier*. 1st ed. Gerald, MO: Patrice Press, 1985.

Glasse, Hannah. *The Art of Cookery Made Plain and Easy*. N.p., 1746.

McDermott, John. "Paincourt to Poverty." *Mid-America Review*, April 5, 1933.

Ministère de la Culture. "La Louisiane Française 1682–1803." culture.gouv. fr/Depot-legal-du-ministere-de-la-Culture.

Missouri Historical Review. "Glimpses of the Past." Missouri Historical Society.

Montigny, de Dumont. *Memoires Historiques sur la Louisiane…*. Paris: Chez Cl. J.B. Bauche, 1753.

Peterson, Charles E. "Life in Colonial St. Louis." Missouri Historical Society, 1949.

Pittman, Philip. *The Present State of the European Settlements on the Mississippi*…. Edited by F.H. Hodder. Cleveland, OH: A.H. Clark Company, 1906.

Primm, Wilson. "New Year's Eve in Olden Time on St. Louis." S. Louis Papers, Missouri Historical Society, 1868.

Scharf, Thomas. *History of St. Louis City and County*. Vol. 2. Philadelphia, PA: L.H. Everts, 1883.

Smelser, Marshall. "The Food Supply of Creole Saint Louis." *Missouri Historical Review* (October 1937).

Chapter 2

Arabia Steamboat Museum. Exhibit materials. steamboats.com/museum/arabia.html.

Arnold, Sam. *Eating Up the Santé Fe*. Chicago: Chicago Review Press, 2001.

Brackenridge, Henry M. *Views of Louisiana, Together with a Journal of a Voyage up the Missouri River in 1811*. Pittsburgh, PA: Cramer, Spear and Eichbaum, 1814.

Burke, Diane Mutti. "Slavery on the Western Border: Missouri's Slave System and Its Collapse during the Civil War." Kansas City Public Library. civilwaronthewesternborder.org/essay.

Bury, Charlotte Campbell. *The Lady's Own Cookery Book*. London: Henry Colburn, 1844.

Carson, Timothy. "Boone's Lick Road History, Boone's Lick Road Association: Following the Trail from Franklin Westward." *Missouri Magazine* (September 15, 2020).

Corbett, Suzanne. *Bingham's River Fare*. Booklet for Saint Louis Art Museum special exhibit, 1989.

———. *Cowpunchers Provisions*. Booklet for Saint Louis Art Museum special exhibit, 1988.

Child, Lydia Maria. Chicken Pie receipt. *The American Frugal Housewife*. Boston: Carter and Hendee, 1830.

Greater Augusta Chamber of Commerce. "History of Augusta." augusta-chamber.org/history.

Gunderson, Mary. *The Food Journal of Lewis & Clark: Recipes of an Expedition*. Yankton, SD: History Cooks, 2003.

Harry S. Truman Presidential Library and Museum archives. Independence, Missouri.

History Uncorked: 200 Hundred Years of Missouri Wine. St. Louis, MO: St. Louis Mercantile Library, 2007.

Hunter-Dawson State Historic Site. General management plan, 2020. New Madrid, Missouri.

Kansas History Society. "Turkey Red Wheat." Kansapedia, March 2011. https://www.kshs.org.

Kirkendall, Richard S. *History of Missouri*. Vol. 5. Columbia: University of Missouri Press, 1986.

Kurlansky, Mark. *Salt: A World History*. London: Penguin Group, 2003.

Mansfield, Leslie. *The Lewis and Clark Cookbook*. Berkeley, CA: Celestial Arts, 2020.

Matson, Madeline. *Food in Missouri: A Cultural Stew*. Columbia: University of Missouri Press, 1994.

Missouri Department of National Resources. dnr.mo.gov.

Missouri Pacific Historical Society Archives. http://www.mopac.org/archives/archives-facility.

Missouri State Archives. "Slavery Echoes: Interviews with Former Missouri Slaves." Federal Writers' Project: Slave Narrative Project. Vol. 10, 1936–38.

Mrs. Putnam's Receipt Book and Young Housekeeper's Assistant. New York: Sheldon, 1869.

National Archives Foundation. "Cooking Club." archivesfoundation.org/cooking-club.

National Park Service Gateway Arch. Site brochures and interpretive materials, 2018–20.

Papers of Ulysses S. Grant. Vol. 1, 1837–61. Mississippi State University Libraries Digital Collections.

Quaker Oats Company Archives. "Aunt Jemima History." quakeroats.com/about-quaker-oats/quaker-history.

Ralat, Jose. "The Food Journals of Lewis and Clark." *Cowboys and Indians* (June 2, 2015).

Randolph, Mary. *The Virginia Housewife*. Washington, D.C.: Davis and Force, 1824.

Ronda, James. *Voyages of Discovery: Essays on the Lewis and Clark Expedition*. Lincoln: University of Nebraska Press, 1984.

Russell, Dakota. "Freedom on the Nathan Boone Farm." Association of Missouri Interpreters Conference, 2011.

Satterfield, Archie. "Missouri's Rhineland." *Chicago Tribune*, May 8, 2000.

Simon, John Y., ed. *The Personal Memoirs of Julia Dent Grant*. Carbondale: Southern Illinois University Press, 1988.
We Proceeded On. The official newsletter of Lewis and Clark Trail Heritage Foundation, August 2001.

Chapter 3

American-Rails. american-rails.com.com.
Fried, Stephen. *Appetite for American*. New York: Random House, 2011.
Hagood, J.H., and R. Hagood. *The Story of Hannibal*. Hannibal, MO: Standard Printing Company, 1976.
Missouri History Museum, Library Archives. Menu collection.
Missouri Life. "Woodside Respite." April 4, 2015. missourilife.com.
Missouri Pacific Railroad Archives. mopac.org/archives.
Missouri State Fair Archives. Missouri Department of Agriculture.
Missouri State Fair 2021 Premium Book. Missouri Department of Agriculture.
National Park Service. National Register of Historic Places.
National Rail Museum. "Tidbits from the Dining Car." nationalrrmuseum.org.
Porterfield, James D. *Dining by Rail*. New York: St. Martin's Press, 1998.
The State Historical Society of Missouri, Digital Collections, www.shsmo.org.
Union Pacific Dining Car Cookbook. Union Pacific Archives, company publication manual.
Vaccaro, Pamela J. *Beyond the Ice Cream Cone: The Whole Scoop on Food at the 1904 World's Fair*. St. Louis, MO: Enid Press, 2004.
Whitaker, Jan. Restaurant-ing through History, August 31, 2010. restaurant-ingthroughhhistory.com.

Chapter 4

Bolin, Margaret Maret. *The Route 66 St. Louis Cookbook*. St. Louis, MO: St. Louis Transitions, 2009.
Dicke, Tom. "Red Gold of the Ozarks: The Rise and Decline of Tomato Canning, 1885–1955. " *Agricultural History* 79, no. 1 (2005): 1–26.
Dufur, Brett. *Exploring Missouri Wine Country*. Rocheport, MO: Pebble Publishing, 1997.

Duncan, Luella. *The Way It Was in Southeast Missouri*. Cape Girardeu, MO: Center for Regional History, Southeast Missouri State University, 2013.

Feast. "The Kings of Kansas City Barbecue." August 25, 2017.

Fiedler, David. *The Enemy Among Us: POWs in Missouri During World War II*. St. Louis: Missouri Historical Society Press and D.W. Fiedler LLC, 2010.

Kansas City Evening Star. "The Grand Barbecue in Progress Today at the South End." September 18, 1880.

KCUR 89. 3. "Meet the Black Entrepreneur Who Created Kansas City Barbecue in the Early 1900s." February 13, 2021.

News-Tribune. "Locals Reflect on Anniversary of Prohibition in Jefferson City." January 18, 2020.

Ozarks Watch. "Consequences of Moonshining in Southern Christian County" (Spring/Summer 2019).

Paris of the Plains: Jazz in Kansas City. Clinton, NY: Fillius Jazz Archive and the Digital Humanities Initiative (DHi), Hamilton College.

Peek, Dan William, and Kent Van Landuyt. *A People's History of the Lake of the Ozarks*. Charleston, SC: The History Press, 2016.

Simonson, John. *Prohibition in Kansas City, Missouri: Highballs, Spooners & Crooked Dice*. Charleston, SC: The History Press, 2018.

St. Louis Globe-Democrat. "3,000 Beer Flats Here, Dillon's Guess." December 24, 1931.

St. Louis Magazine. "The Best St. Louis Jazz Musicians of All Time." June 1, 2012.

St. Louis Post-Dispatch. "The Home of the Throwed Rolls." June 9, 1991.

———. "A Look Back: 5,000 Settle in Shacks Along the Mississippi During the Great Depression." January 14, 2019.

———. "Prohibition Dealt a Blow to St. Louis Breweries." September 23, 2011.

———. "6,000 Gallons of Beer Seized in Brewery." May 27, 1932.

Taylor, Candacy. *Overground Railroad: The Green Book and the Roots of Black Travel in America*. New York: Abrams Press, 2020.

U.S. Department of the Interior. National Register of Historic Places Registration Form: Seven-Up Company Headquarters, January 7, 2004.

Chapter 5

Feast. "How David Leong Invented Springfield-Style Cashew Chicken." March 27, 2015.

Kansas City Business Journal. "The Man Behind Kansas City's Craft Cocktail Movement: Ryan Maybee." February 8, 2012.

Riverfront Times. "It's Official: St. Louis Leads the Nation in Pork Steak Purchases." May 26, 2017.

Smithsonian. "A Brief History of the Crock Pot." November 26, 2019.

St. Louis Post-Dispatch. "Hoffmanns Acquire Augusta, Missouri, Assets and Businesses." January 4, 2021.

———. "Spring in the Atrium," April 5, 1987.

INDEX

ABOUT THE AUTHORS

Suzanne Corbett is an award-winning writer, culinary teacher and food historian whose work has appeared in local and national publications. She is the author of *The Gilded Table: Recipes and Table History from the Campbell House, Pushcarts & Stalls: The Soulard Market History Cookbook* and *Unique Eats and Eateries of St. Louis.* She is also a Telly Award–winning producer/writer of the documentary short *Vintage Missouri: 200 Years of Missouri Wine.* She serves as a foodways interpreter and research food historian with the National Park Service's Gateway Arch National Park and the Ulysses S. Grant National Historic Site, in addition to sites in French Colonial Ste. Geneviève. In addition, she has appeared as a guest lecturer and interpreter at numerous historic sites and organizations throughout the United States. Suzanne has a master's degree in media communications from Webster University, is a member of the National Federation of Press Women and the North American Travel Journalists, is a Certified Culinary Professional with the International Association of Culinary Professionals and is a member of the Les Dames d'Escoffier International.

Deborah Reinhardt is a native Missourian and an award-winning travel and food writer. For more than thirty years, Deborah was managing editor of *AAA Midwest Traveler* and *AAA Southern Traveler.* As author of

Delectable Destinations: A Chocolate Lover's Guide to Missouri, Deborah believes the world would be a kinder place if we all ate one piece of good chocolate each day. Her food blog, at ThreeWomenintheKitchen.com, in 2021 was awarded first place in the personal category by the National Federation of Press Women. She self-published a family cookbook, *Three Women in the Kitchen: Recipes and Stories of Growing Up in St. Louis,* in 2021 and is donating all proceeds to Circle of Concern food pantry. She is co-president of Missouri Professional  Communicators, the Missouri affiliate of the National Federation of Press Women, as well as a member of the St. Louis Culinary Society. Deborah is a journalism graduate of Southern Illinois University–Edwardsville.